To Dad,
for showing me that my career
is all what I make of it.

Find the right *now* role.

Find the right now role.

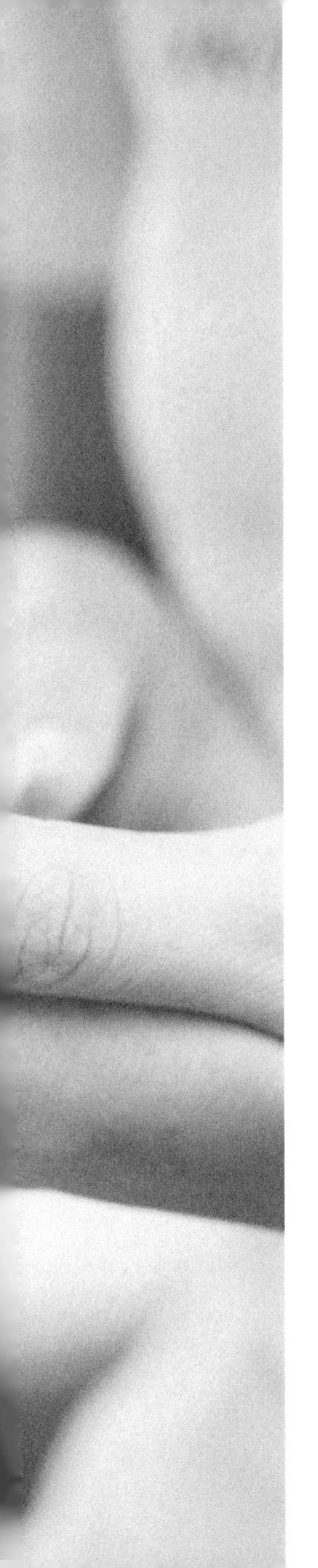

I never thought this would be me. I had delivered 'the call' many times, read from the script, explained the next steps... but never did I think I would receive one. But now it was me... and I quickly learned, my actions in the next hours and days would say a lot about who I am as a leader.

Find the Right Now Role

Your existing team needs you... more than ever. There may be people impacted next to you, above you and alongside you. Then there will be associates wondering what is next. While you are focused on being strong for you, remember they are all still watching you... and you need to still be strong for them because while it is happening to you... it is happening to them too.

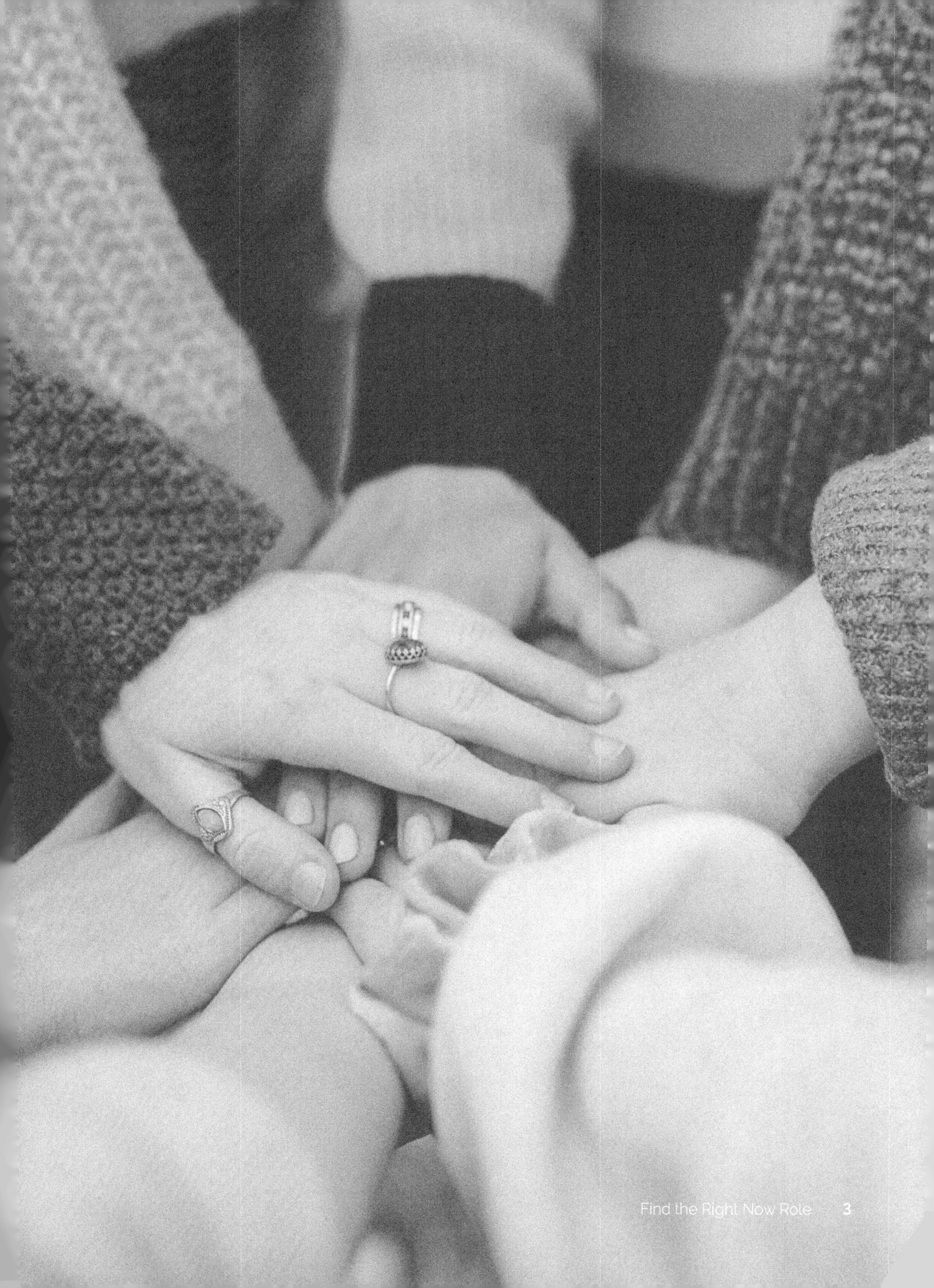

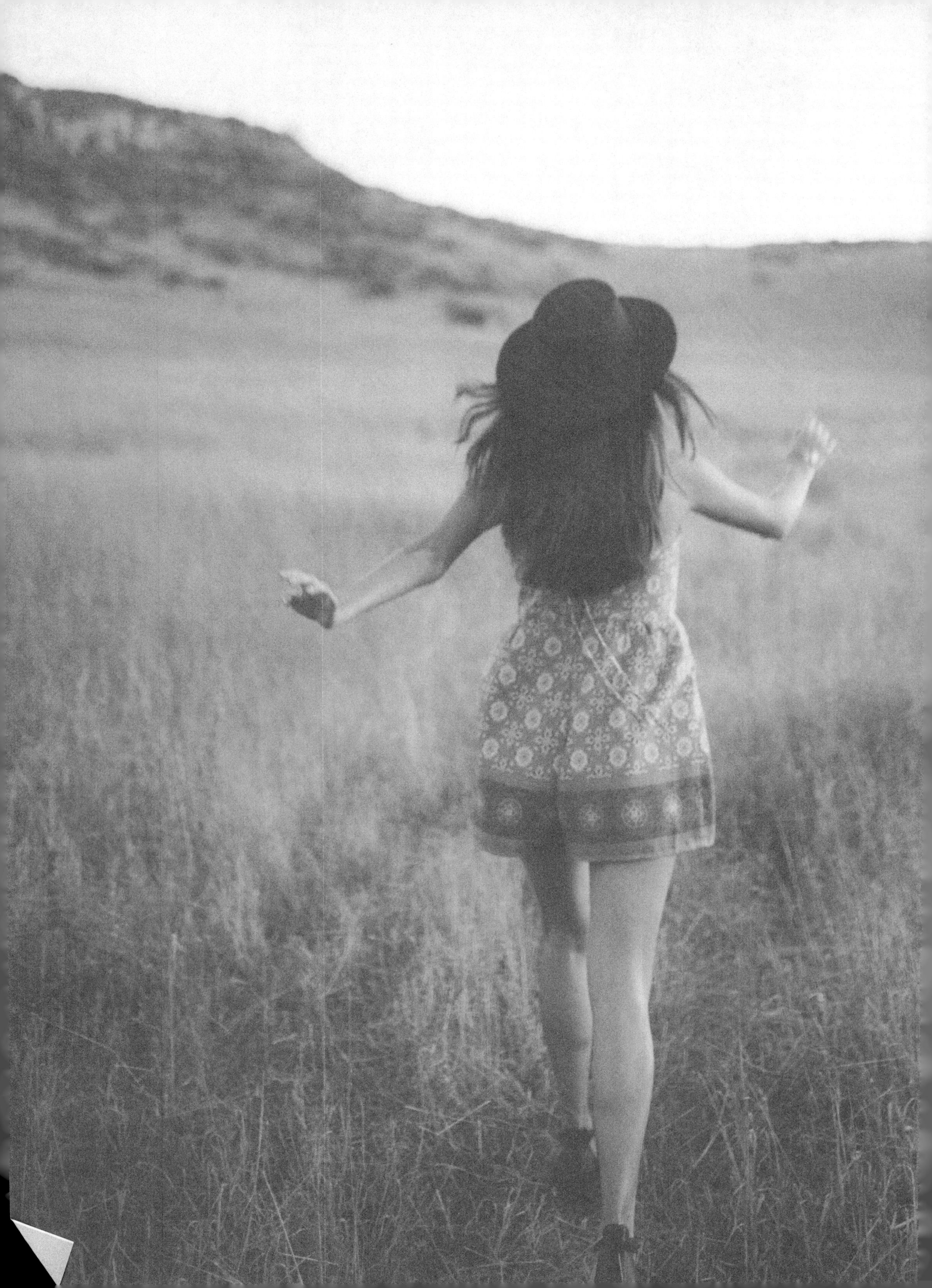

You can exit gracefully. I held my head high, I graciously offered to assist and help the new team transition. I knew the very best me was going to leave a career of almost two decades... because that is not only the leader that I wanted to be, it was the leader I am.

What if you want to leave but are waiting for an exit strategy... you can still start now. Blow up your network, find forums and opportunities to connect with people at companies you admire. Search out people who recently took a new role... learn more about their paths and 'how' they moved to their latest role.

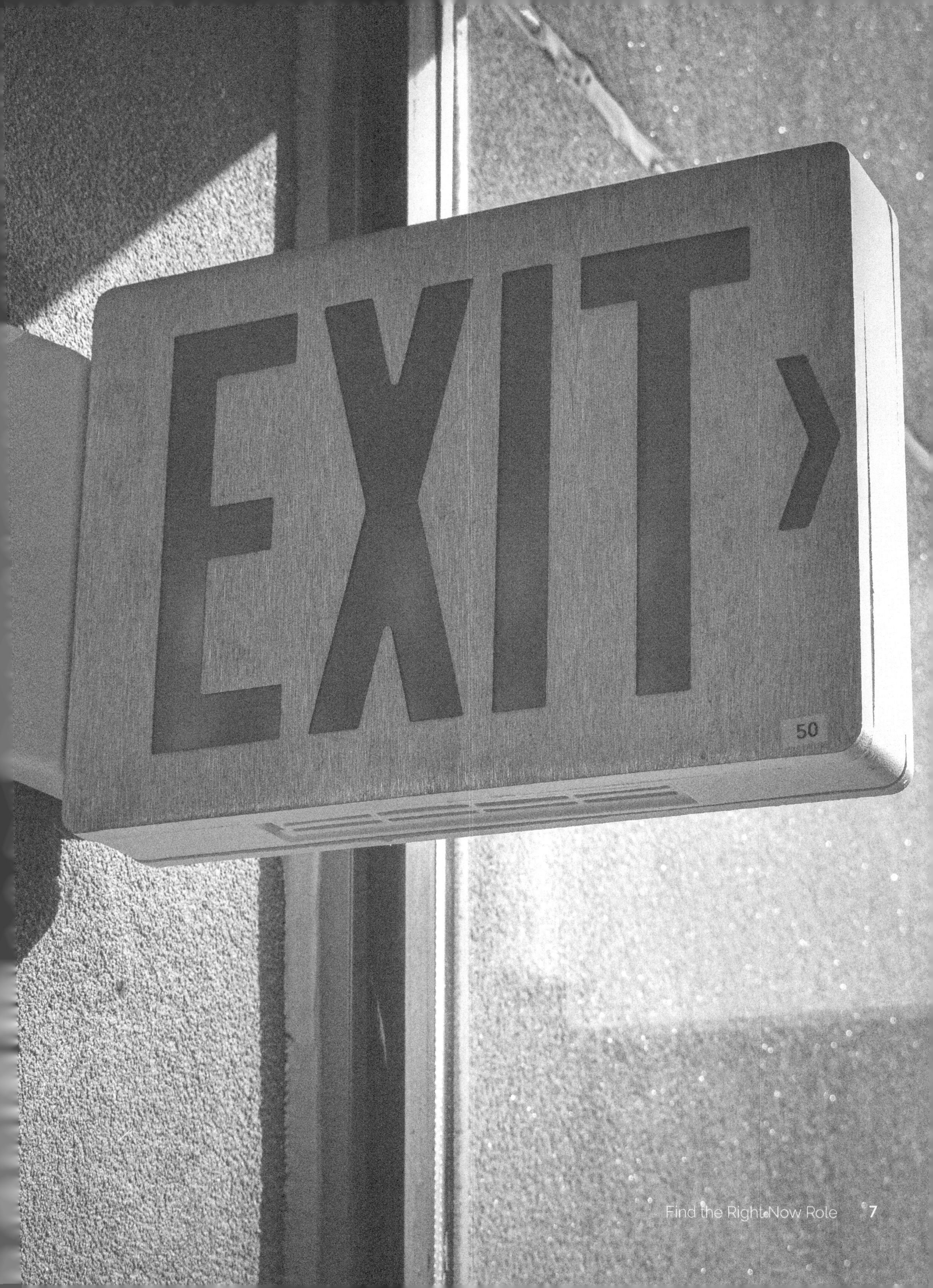
EXIT
50

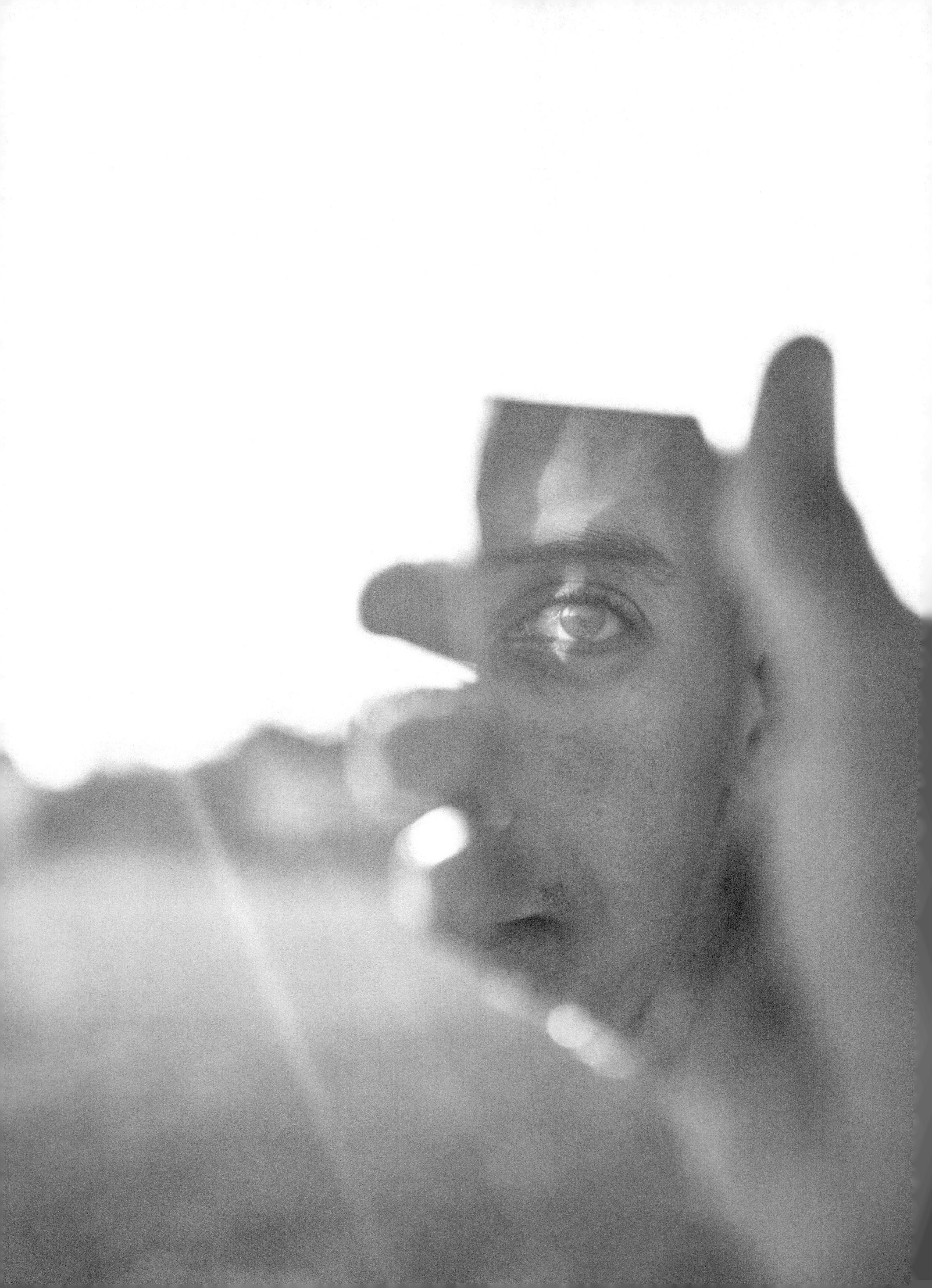

You need to make it about you every day. I received great advice from a fellow leader early in the process... 'They made their choice... now you need to choose you." Wow, in all my years, I would choose my team, my boss, the business and our customers... but I rarely practiced choosing me. What a great wake up call that everyday going forward was now about what was best for me.

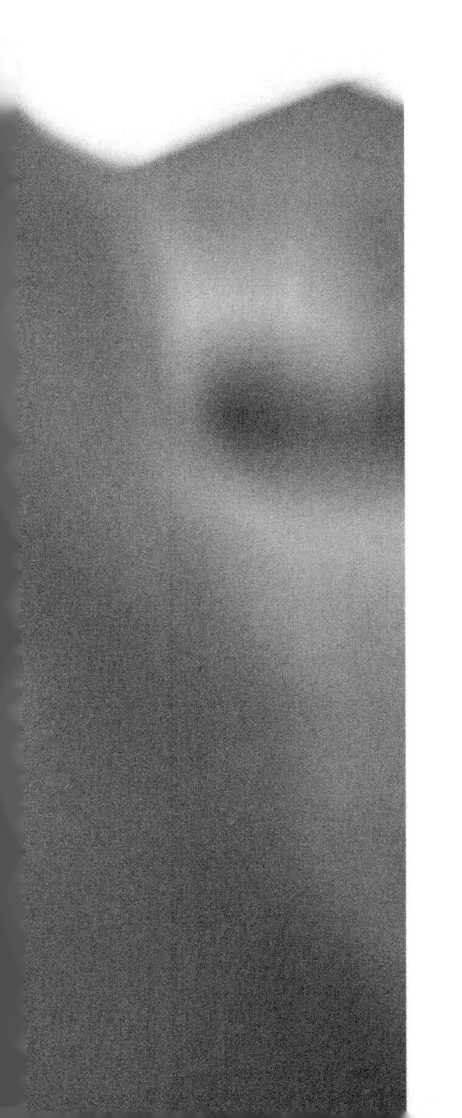

Spend time on your finances... if you don't have a financial planner get one. Get clear on what expenses you can defer, minimize or cut out. Make a plan for what your financial timeline looks like and solve for insurance.

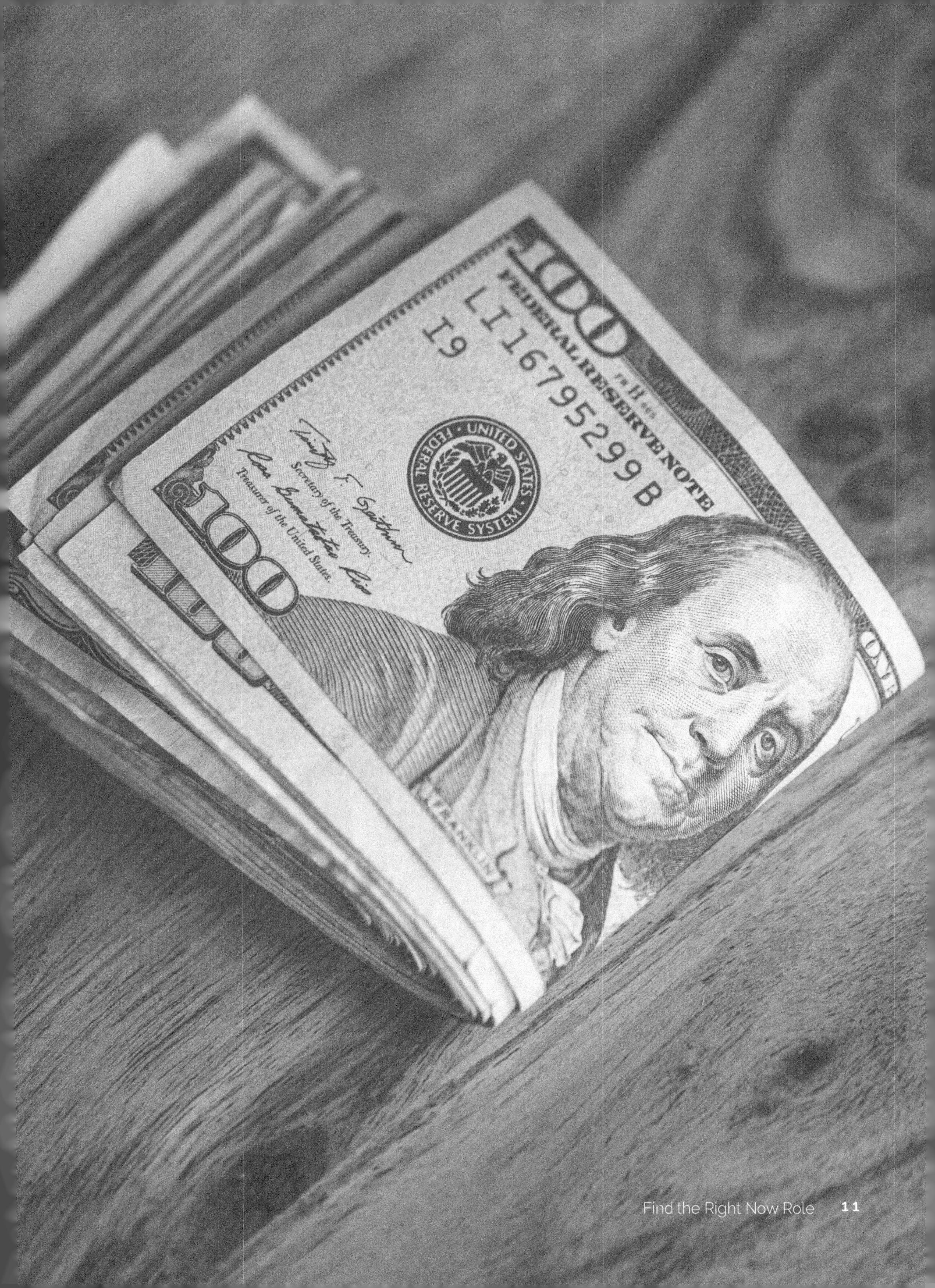

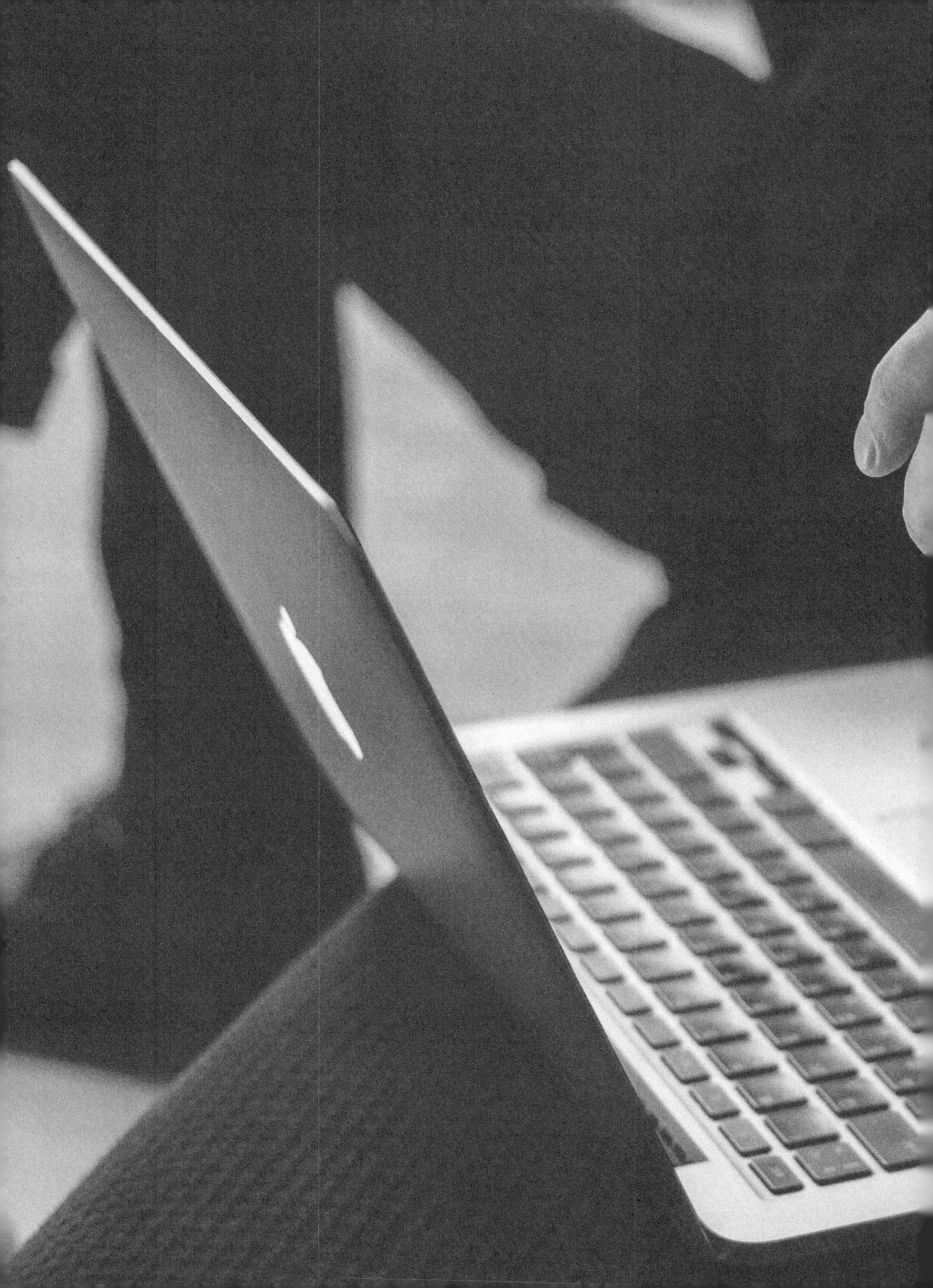

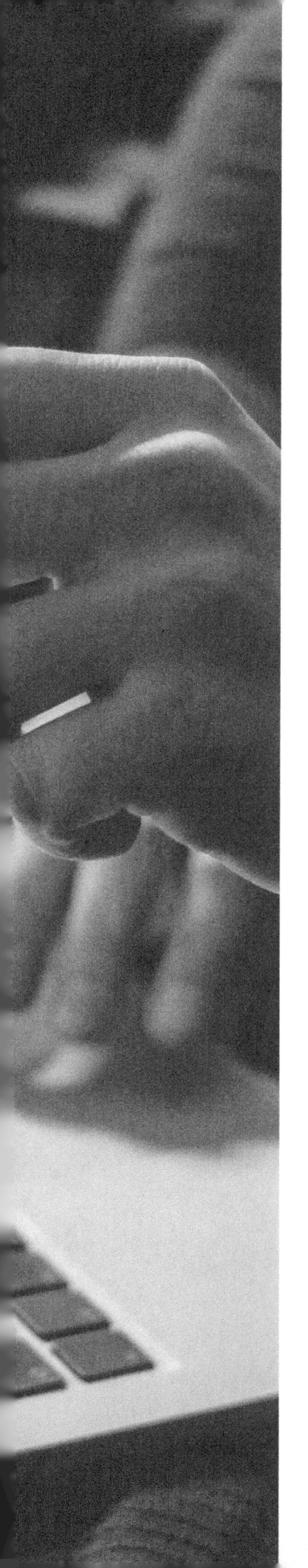

Invest in your own personal devices. I know I may not be alone... when I started my recent career search I purchased my first personal computer, ever (and purchasing them for teenagers doesn't count). Set up all your personal information that may have been linked via your work laptop. You will appreciate doing this asap so you are functioning on day one.

You find out who your real 'work' friends are... and it isn't everyone you thought. From the moment of the announcement, the people who wanted to help and just let me know they were thinking of me, reached out in droves... and others... they didn't. Was a great lesson for me, even a few words of encouragement as people leave their roles, is very much appreciated.

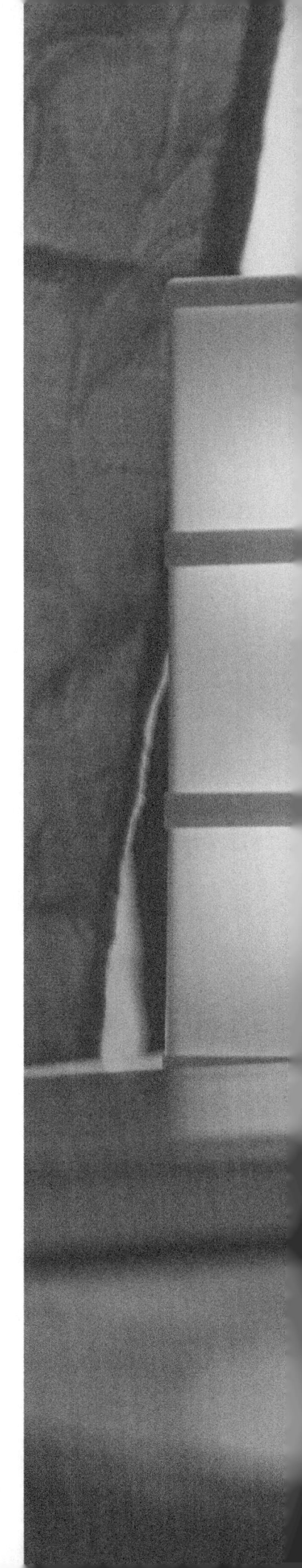

Find the Right Now Role

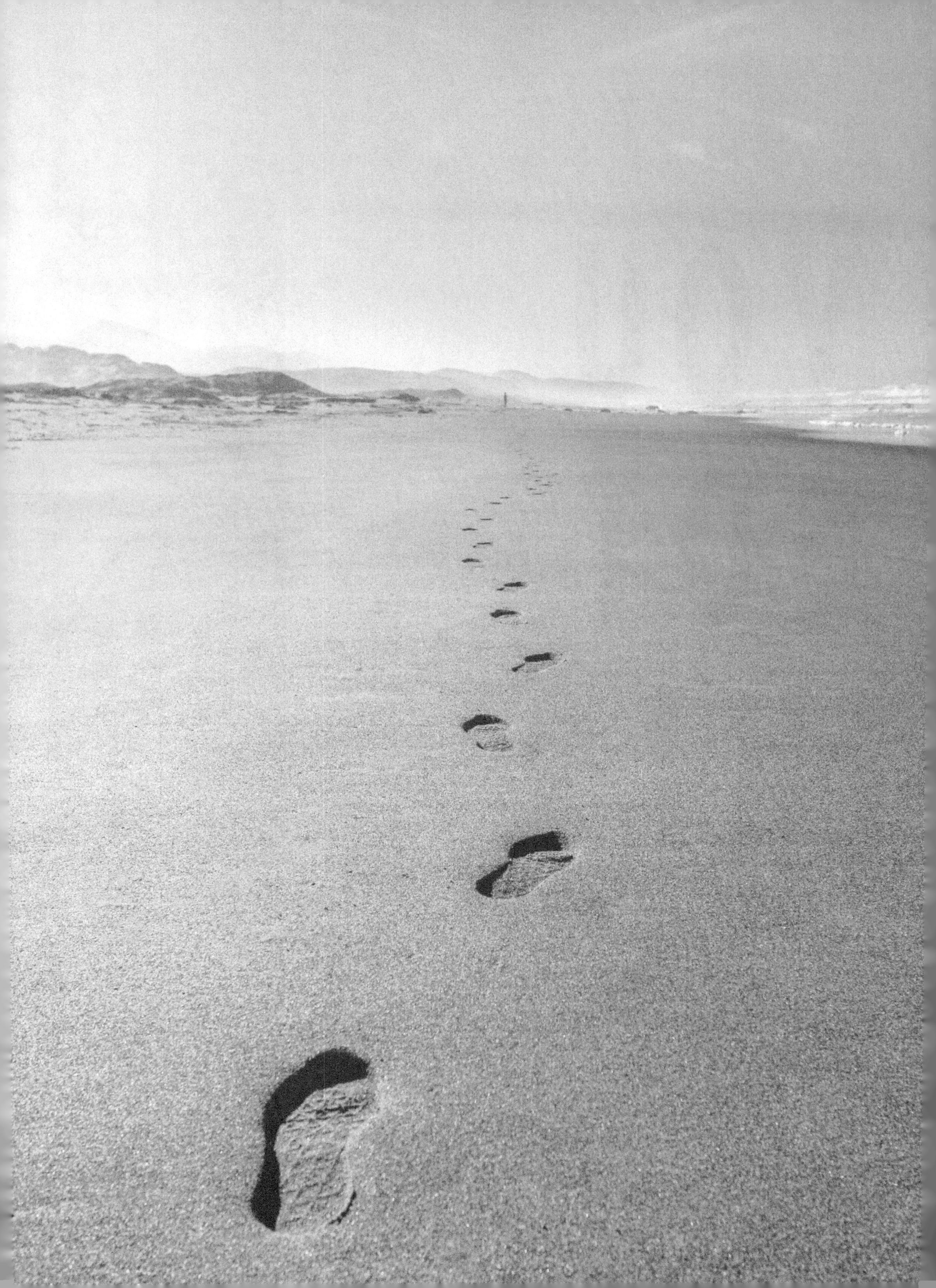

You will be missed... but not like you think. For all the initiatives and programs I led and executed, I quickly learned few would miss 'what' I did, but would comment they missed 'how' I did it. This was a great reminder for me to focus on what was important to me as a leader.

Deepen your relationships with your mentors and close advisors who will help you 'keep it real' during the journey. These are the people who will give you the space and grace to 'Be Real' (like the app!). You can say it like it is, good and bad, and they will walk alongside you all the way.

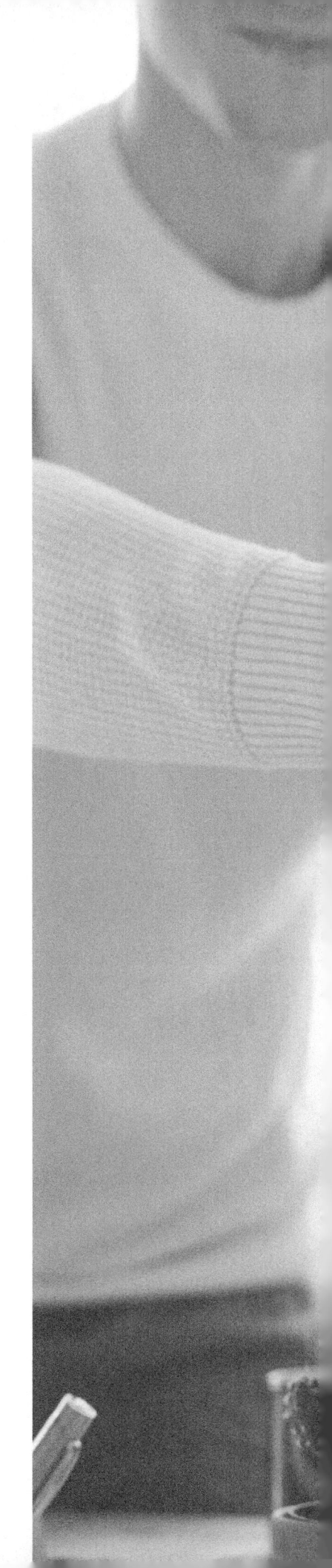

Find the Right Now Role 19

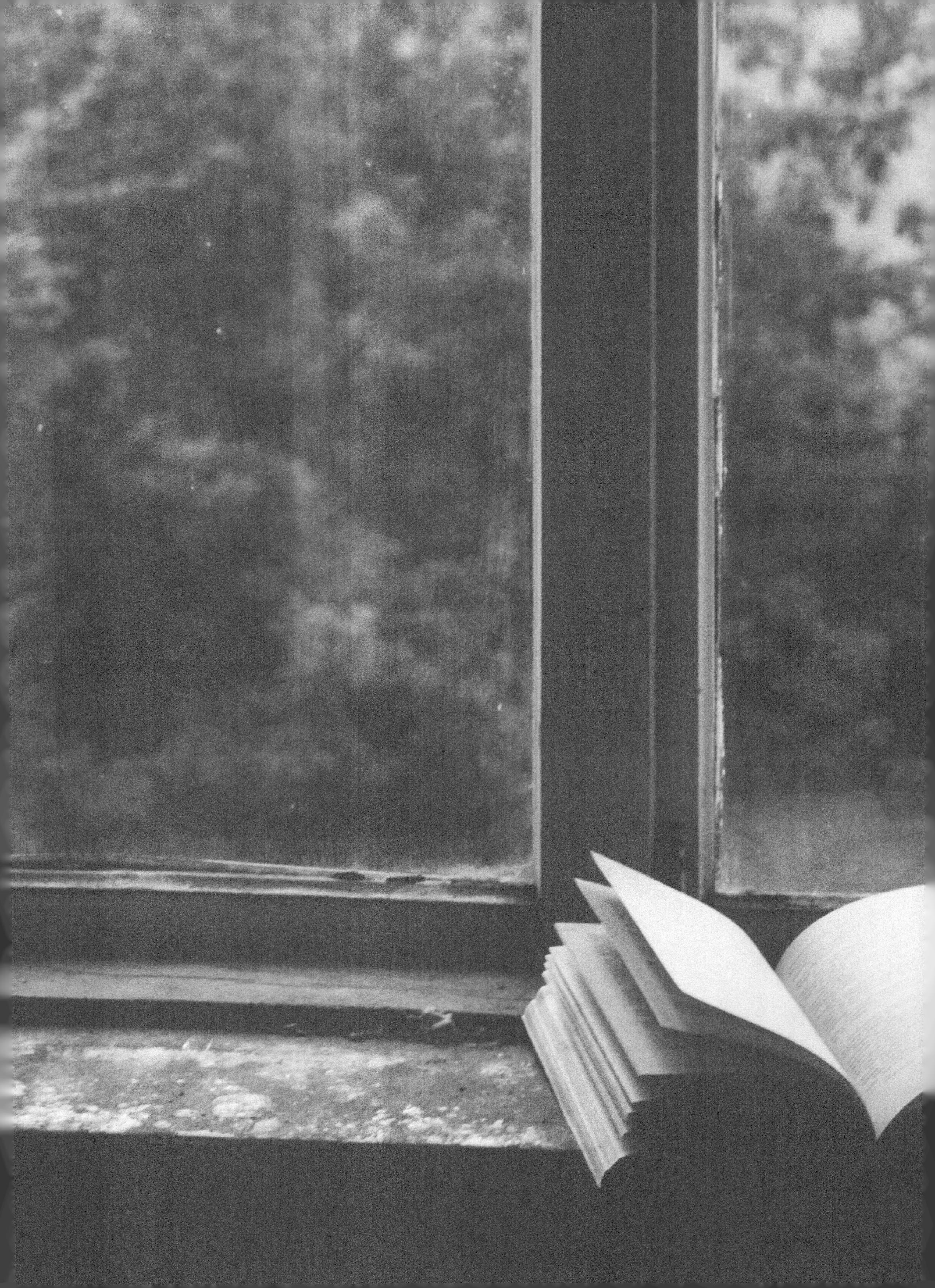

There isn't a handbook for this. No one writes a book and tells you... this is how they leave a job. So let me give me you the cliff notes:

1) Hold your head high,
2) Be kind and helpful and
3) Don't burn bridges... even if you are tempted to enact a 'scorched earth policy'.

Take with you what matters most... the chockis on my desk, accolades for integrations delivered and momentos from trips didn't make the cut. What I made sure to pack with me was my leadership style, my open door policy whether I was employed or not, and my humility.

Find the Right Now Role 23

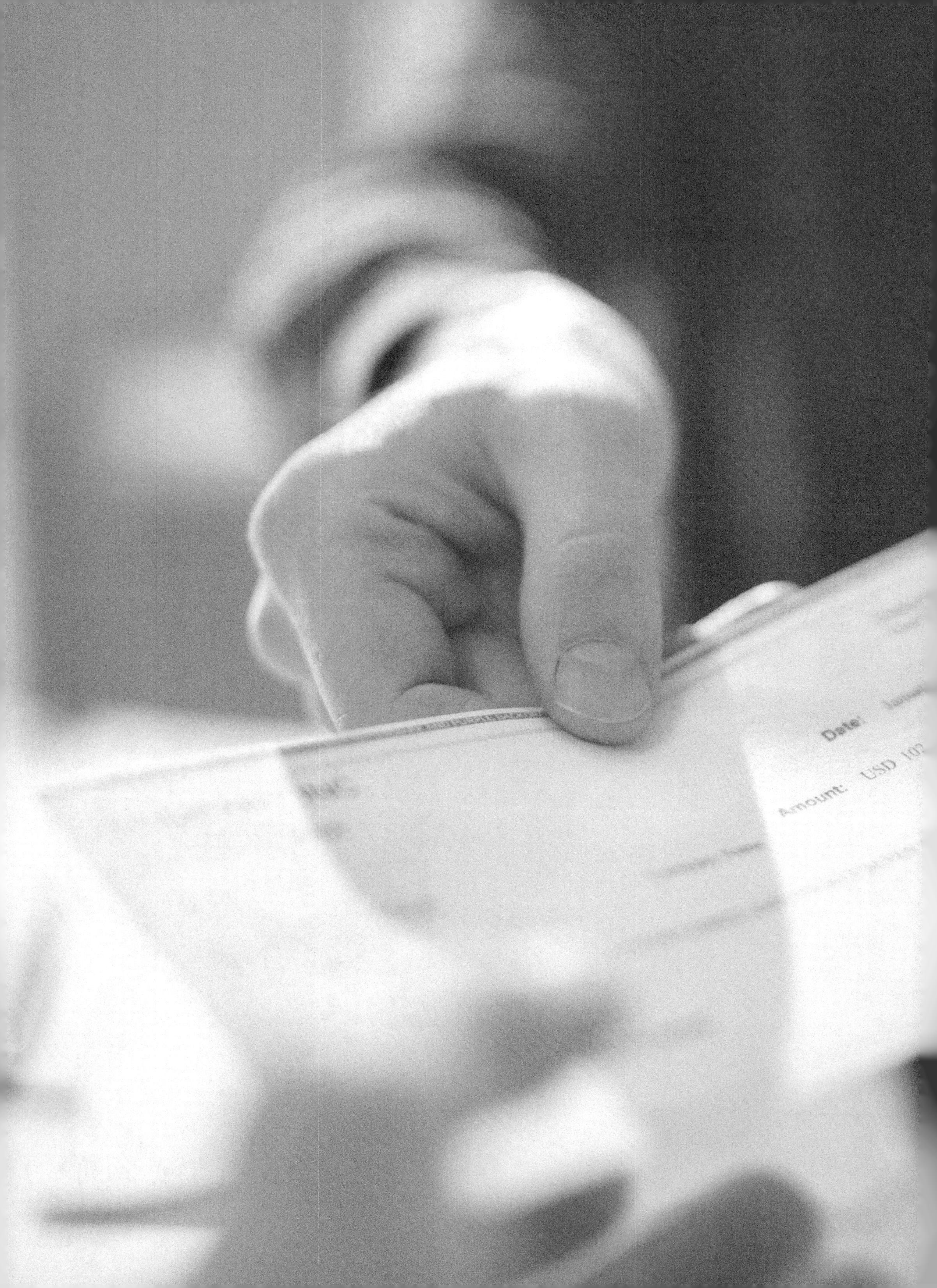
Date:
Amount: USD 102

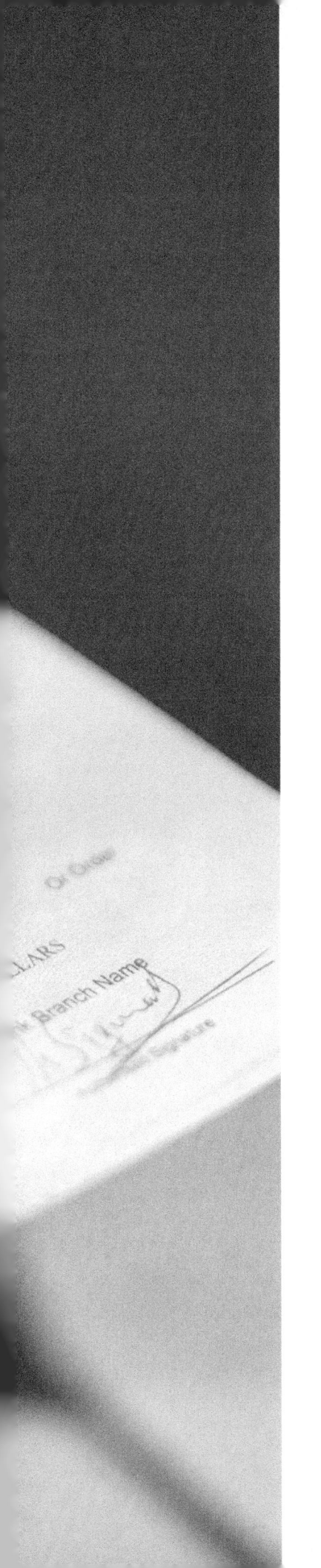

If you stay at a company long enough, there is a high likelihood it will be you one day. Years ago senior people used to counsel me, if you stay long enough... don't leave without a check. While I am not sure that is the best tactic for everyone, it can be an advantage to empower you to use the time to find the right match in your next role.

After your last day, take a moment... like the end of any relationship, the 'transition' phase and being on the other side are very different. Give yourself the space and grace to feel how you feel. Congratulate yourself, it is the first day of the next chapter!

Find the Right Now Role 27

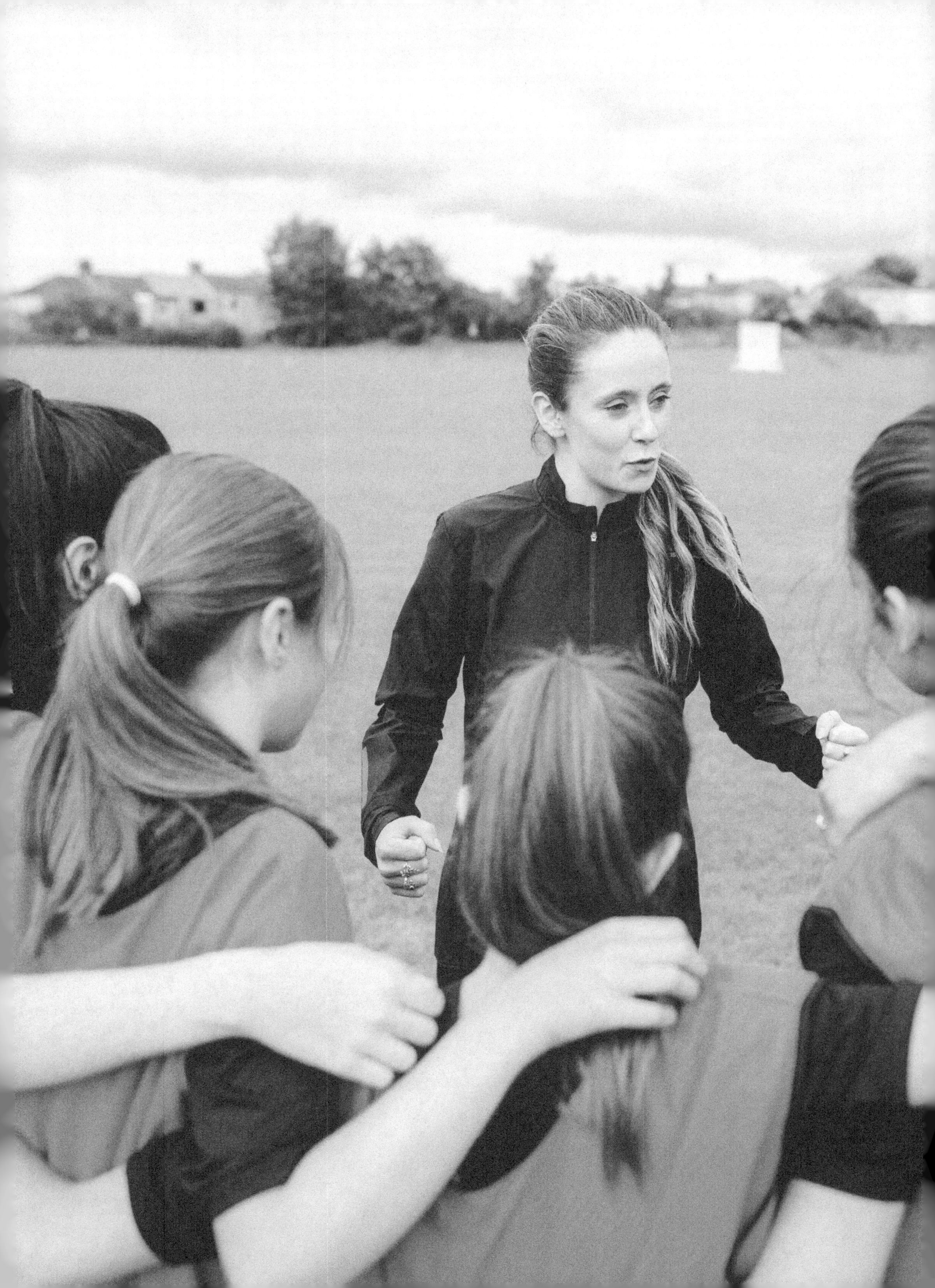

Hire a coach... many of them. Therapist? Life coach? Executive coach? Outplacement coach? I know from first hand experience they can all be helpful in different ways. Surround yourself with people who want to help you get to your dream job. Learn from them and take what speaks to you and apply it.

Outsource some of the foundational work. I quickly learned in the new era of online tools and search processes... there was a way to do this well. Find the people who are experts in resumes, LinkedIn and networking. Invest in you... you get what you pay for... .like a good pair of shoes. Your next role is the biggest investment of time and energy you will make... so put your money into doing it right.

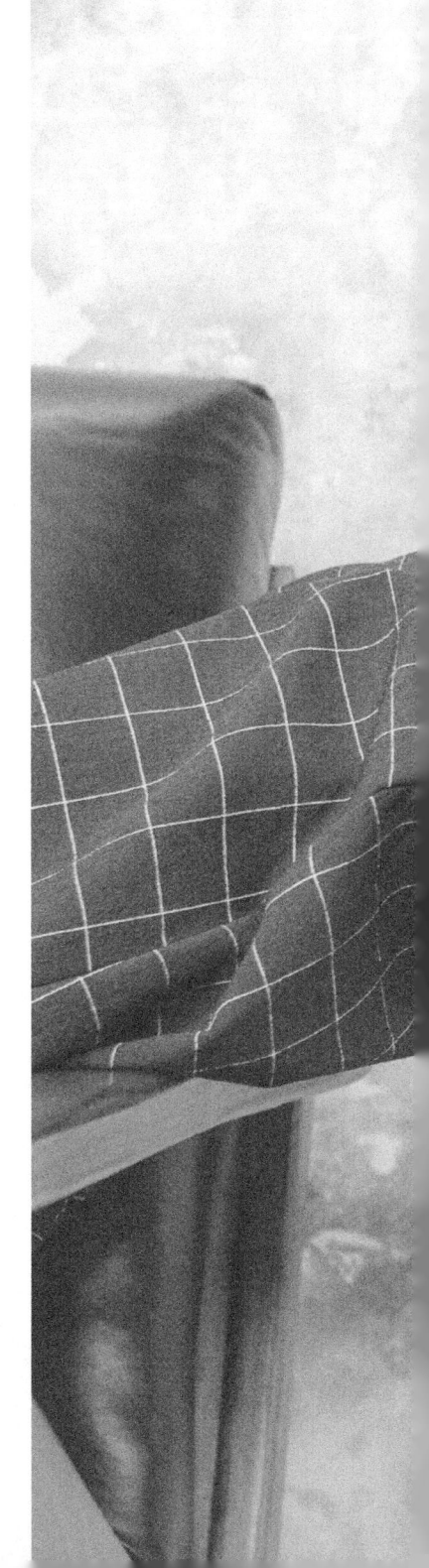

Find the Right Now Role   31

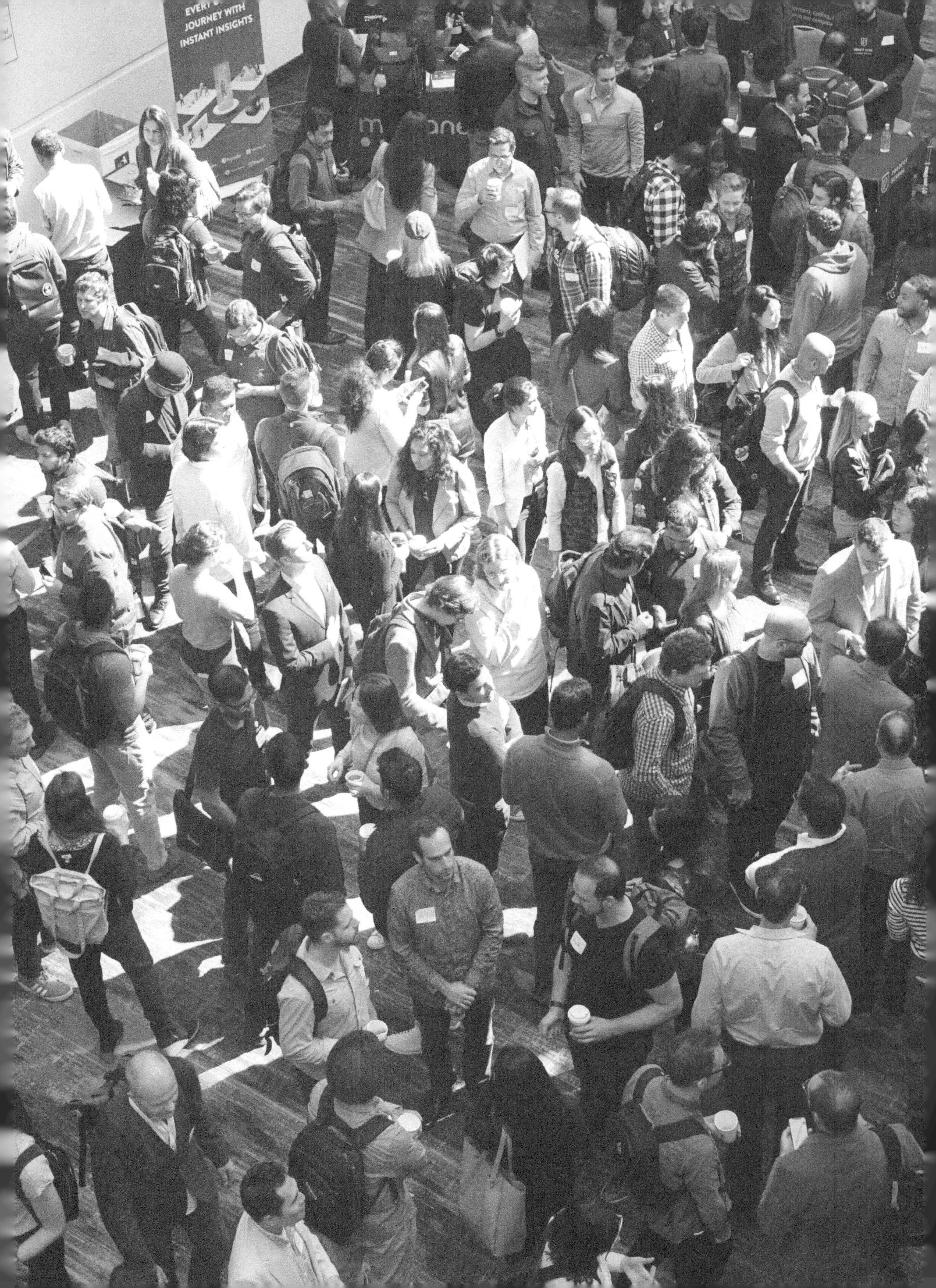
EVERY
JOURNEY WITH
INSTANT INSIGHTS

The highs will be high and the lows will be low... days of wondering 'how will I ever find my next job', days of negative self talk, fear and worry. Only to be offset by the amazing connections, opportunities that show up out of nowhere, and people who come into your orbit like divine intervention.

Find the Right Now Role

Talk to everyone... take every call, answer every 'spam' LinkedIn message... you never know who will lead you to the person, who will lead you to the next person, who will lead you to the person who offers you the role of your dreams.

Find the Right Now Role

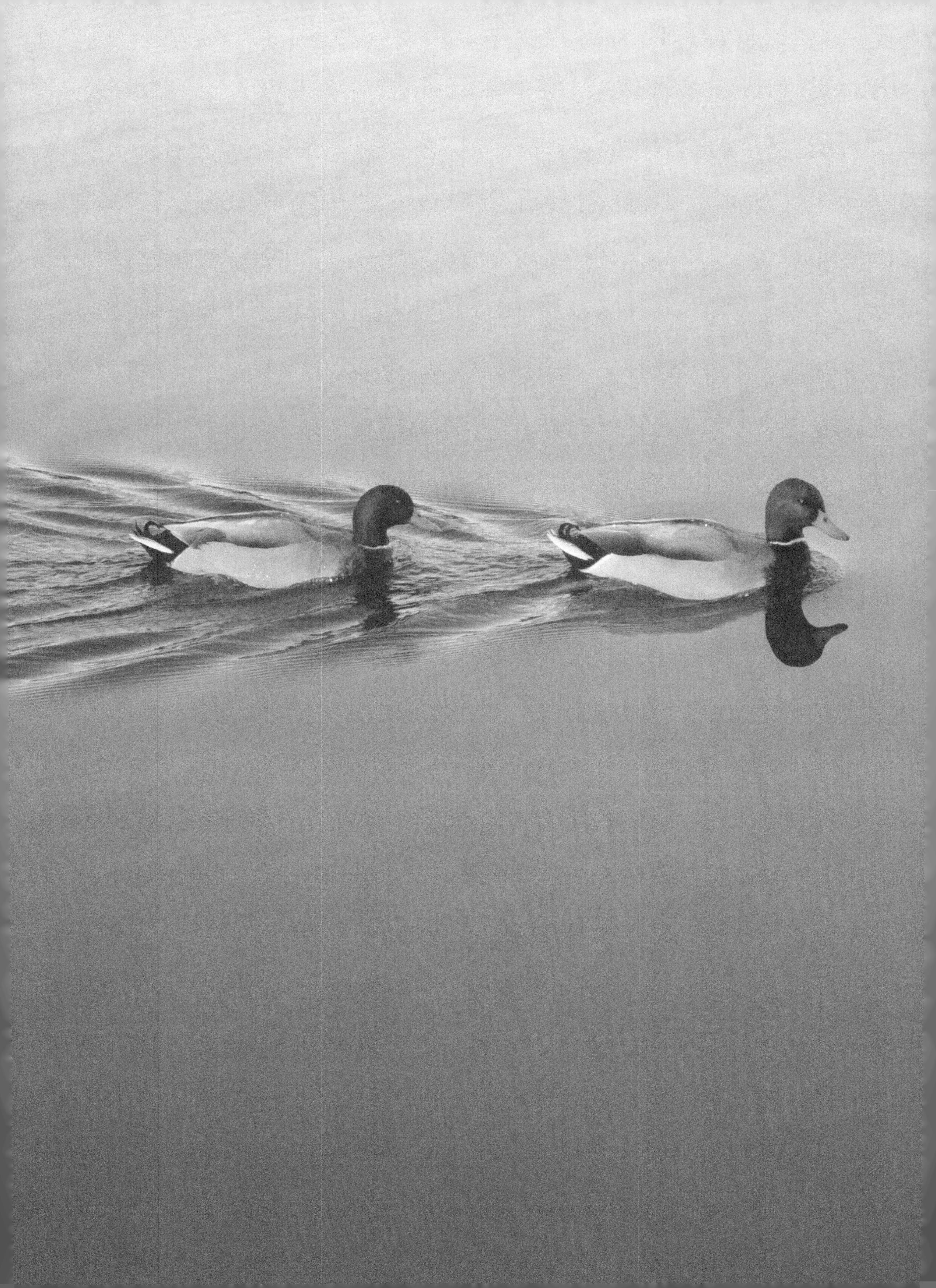

Ask people for advice and guidance on your search, don't ask for a job. Just about anyone is happy to offer advice and ideas on who else in their network may be a good connection for you to make.

Always offer to help the people who agree to meet with you. Leave every conversation with 'how can I assist you'. While you are focused on your next role, it is valuable to offer assistance in return.

Find the Right Now Role   39

Contacts

Keep a list of everyone you talk to, who connected you to them and their contact information. After the first 10 people it will be hard to keep track... believe me it comes in handy months later when you are trying to remember the person who connected you to the person.

All connections are good connections... past colleagues, past bosses from prior companies, friends from high school, college, even grade school, spouses and partners of friends, ex-boyfriends/ex-girlfriends and even reaching out cold to people on LinkedIn....you get the idea. All is fair game in networking... I learned 99.9% of people will get back to you. And it is ok to follow up in a few weeks if they don't... they aren't ignoring you.... they are just busy!

This is my glorious paddle crew who keep me connected in all things big and small.

Find the Right Now Role 43

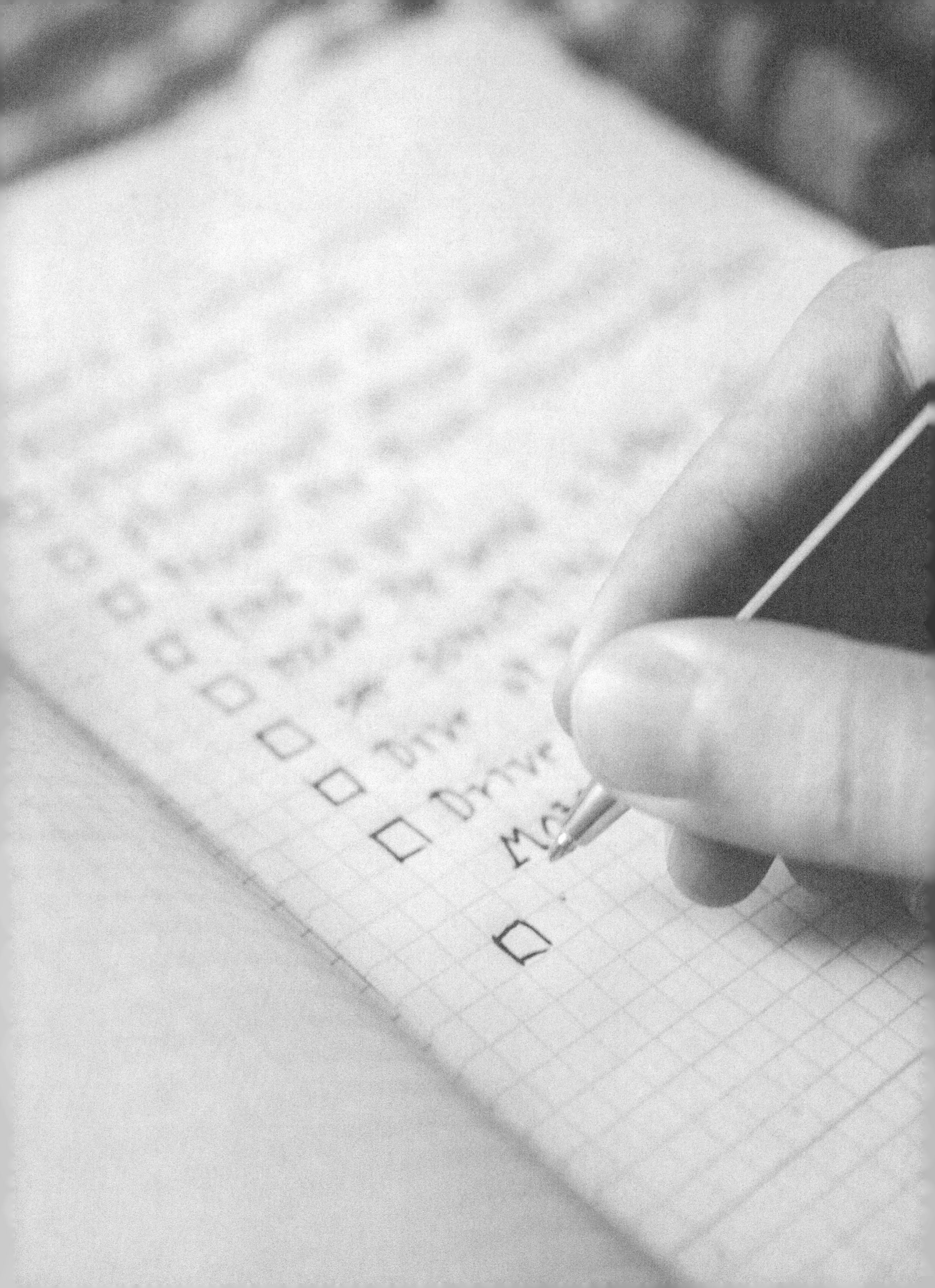

Get really clear on what is important to you... and know it may change during the process and that is ok. Make a list of non-negotiables, nice to haves and 'icing on the cake' qualities. From compensation, to roles, to culture... figure out what you truly want.

Find your grateful... everyday. Find a reason to see joy in the process. Where are there opportunities you wouldn't otherwise have, more time with family and friends, more time for you. Embrace it!

I am thankful my sisters, dad and I were able to reunite at our family cabin, otherwise known as 'the happiest place on earth', for the first time in 30+ years. These memories I was able to create during this special time in my life.

Find the Right Now Role   47

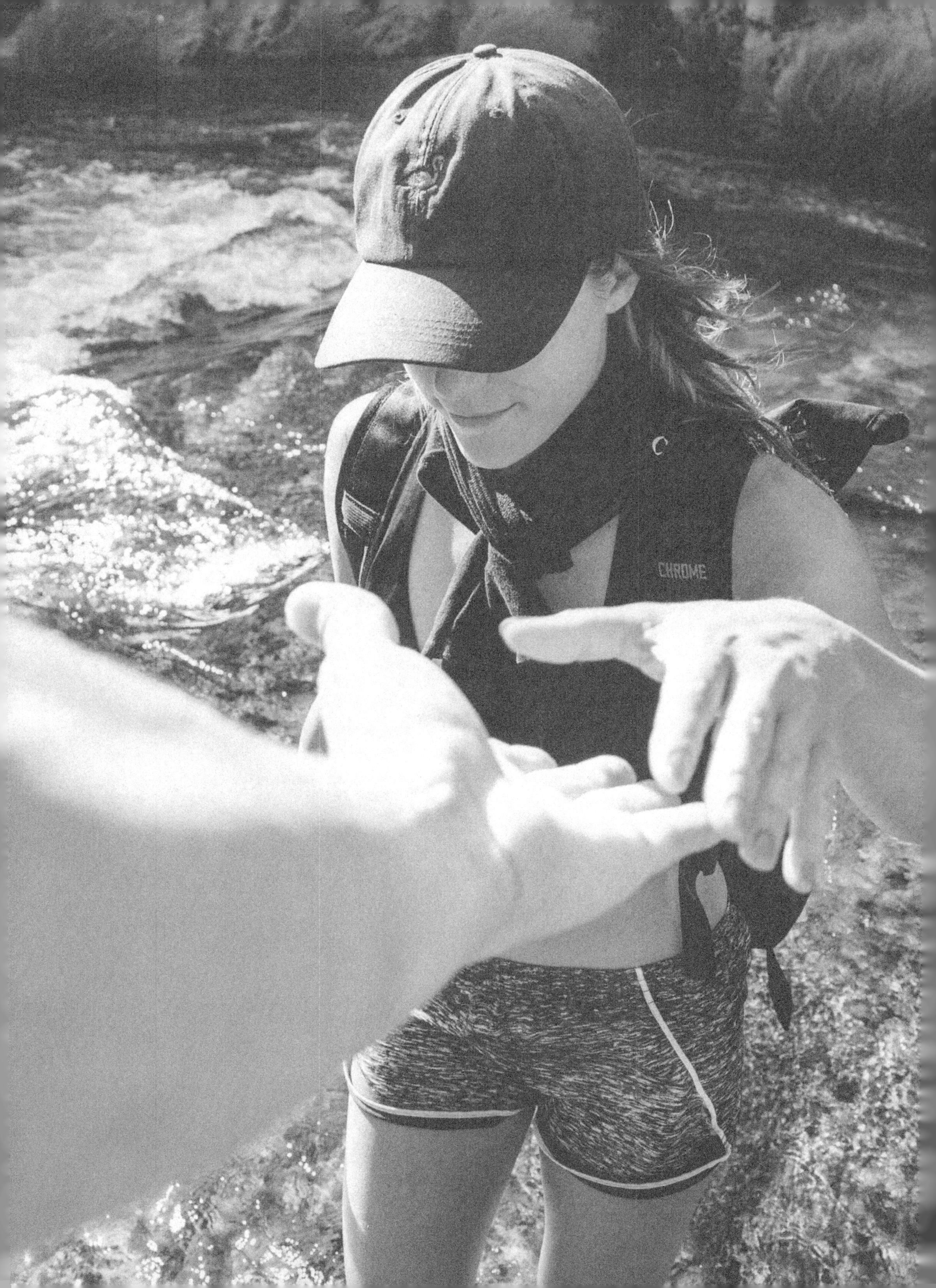
CHROME

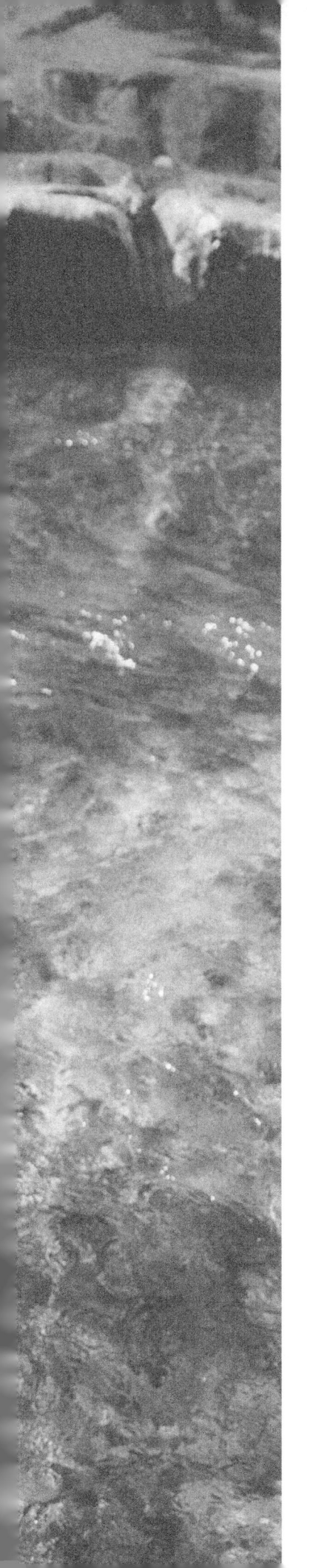

Help others... Three months into my job search process, I had the opportunity to offer advice to someone who was going through a similar experience. I learned a lot about how far I had come as I shared recruiter contacts, resume writers and coaches. Be the person you wish you had when you started.

Your job is not your identity. Read that again. For me that meant, figuring out who I was without having the title. I love the quote 'Lead in a way that your team would want to follow you without the title'.

Find the Right Now Role 51

Are you going to own the pen to the story you are writing?

I am partial to pens... I like good ones (if you know you know). I have learned that, more than the pen, I need to own my story including the narrative for today and tomorrow. I own how I feel, my choices and how I learn from them. The most fun part....there is always more to write!

Do you know where are you headed… some days I know exactly where I am going and how to get there. Other days I have a general gut feel and follow it. Still others I have moments of 'Where am a I?' Regardless of the day or moment, I stay true to me, what aligns with my passions, my goals and what feels good. Even when I am walking on my treadmill to nowhere… I am grounded in where I am headed.

Find the Right Now Role

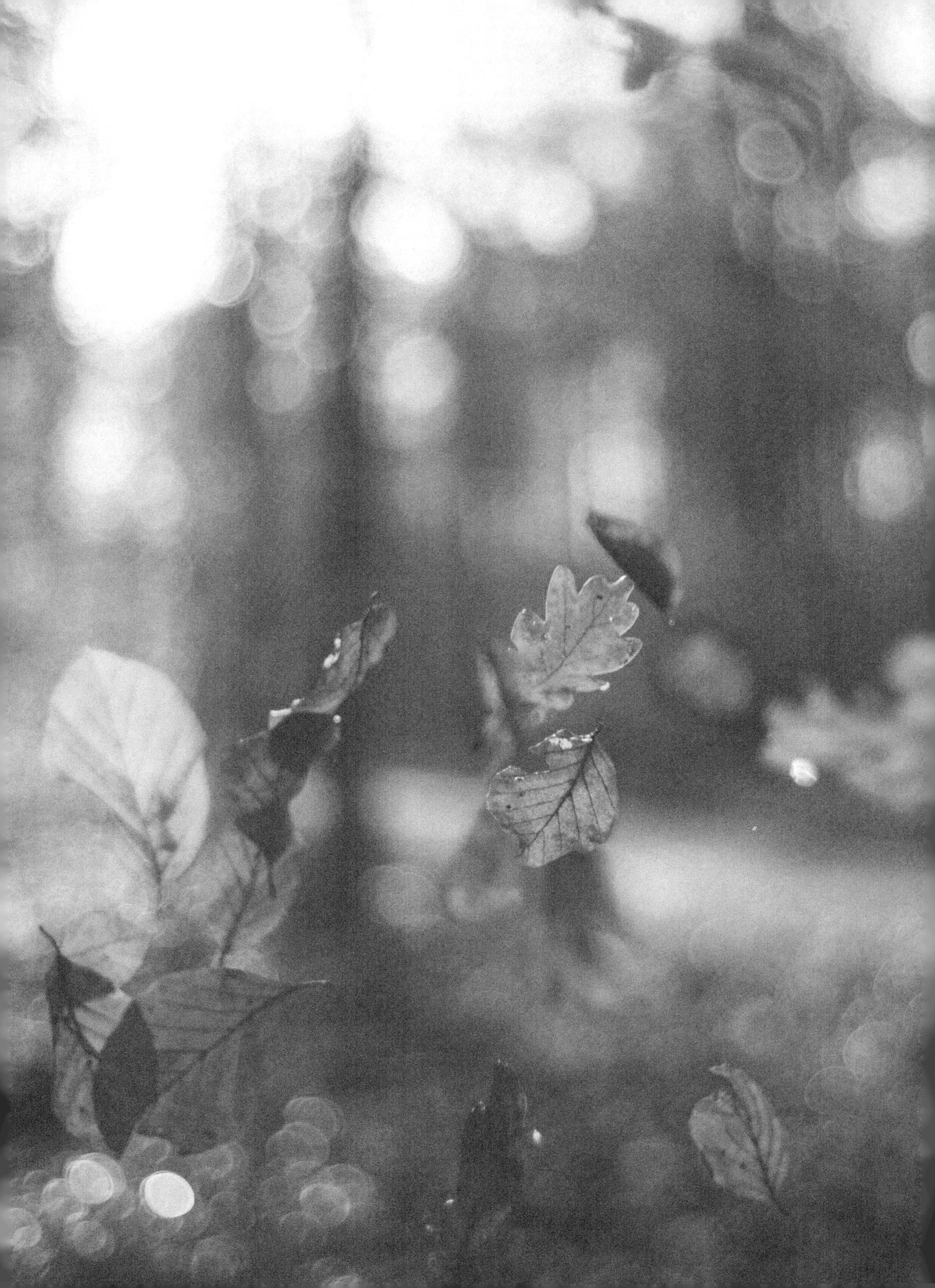

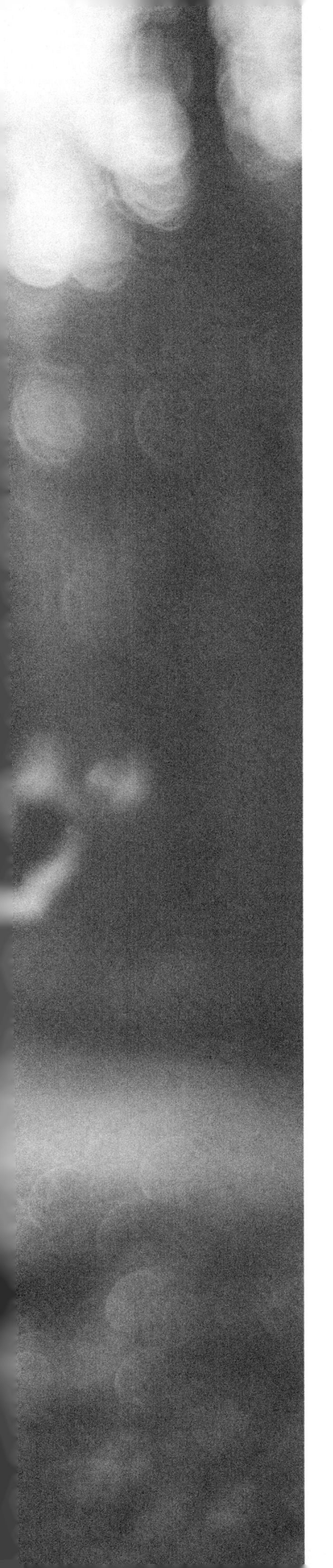

How do you process change and transition in your life? I have learned when I spend the time to focus on how I feel in the moment I can let go of what isn't serving me and make space for new, expanded and bigger opportunities. As I watch the leaves change and fall, I am reminding myself that change brings clarity and growth.

The only way through is through... well sometimes. But often you need to go over, under, around or just leap frog the whole thing to get to where you want to go. So before you charge ahead... ask yourself if there is another path you can take?

Find the Right Now Role 59

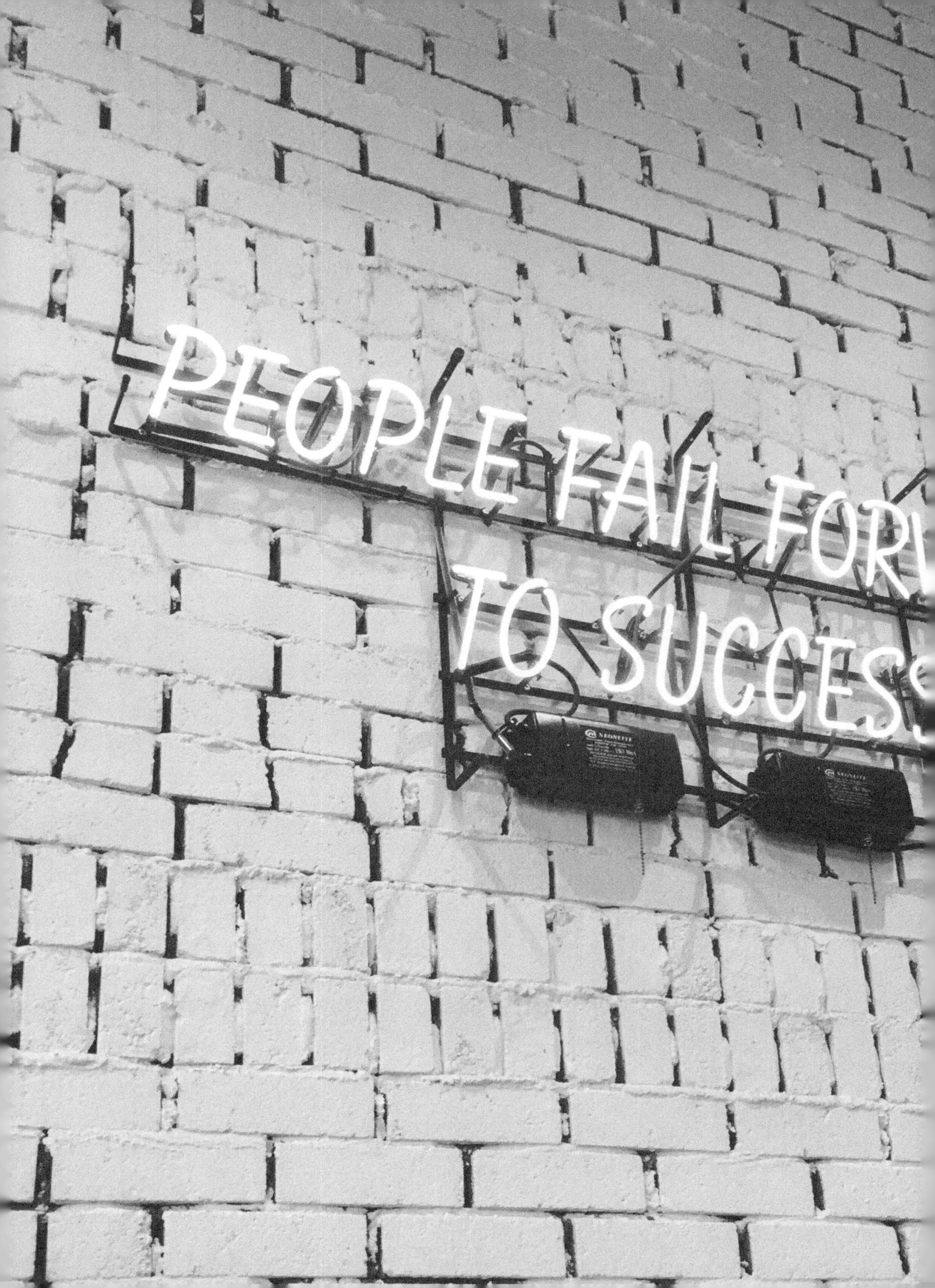
PEOPLE FAIL FOR
TO SUCCES

Can you fail up? Why do we always think that a failure is falling down? A dear friend and I always used to look at those people who failed up and wondered what the heck do they know that we don't? Well they probably don't take themselves too seriously, they don't wallow in it and they don't see it as a fail. The 'fail uppers' do see the opportunity, they do take risks, and they do move on. Who wants to be a 'fail upper' with me?

There are elevator pitches but do you have a tag line pitch? We have all been told to craft a sixty second pitch but I have found huge success with a one liner. 'Do great work with great people.' What's yours?

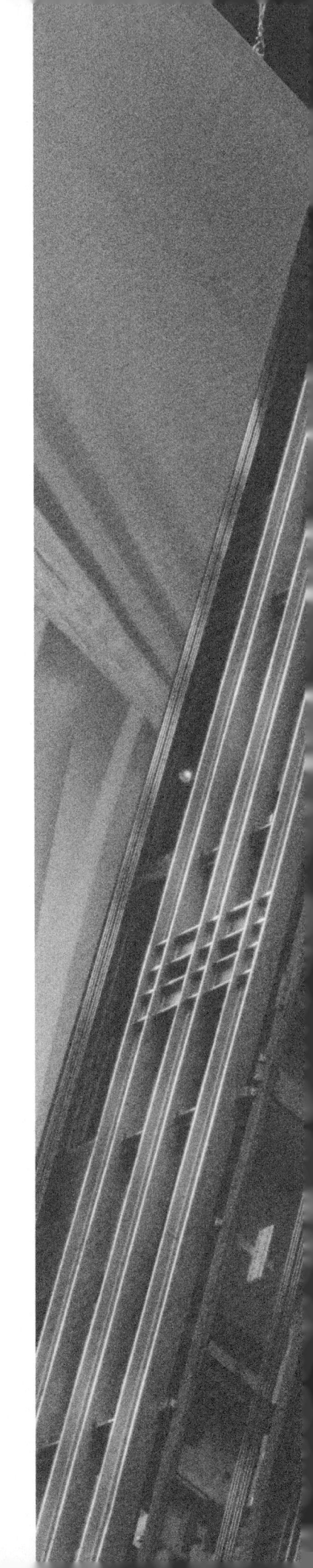

Find the Right Now Role

LET IT GO

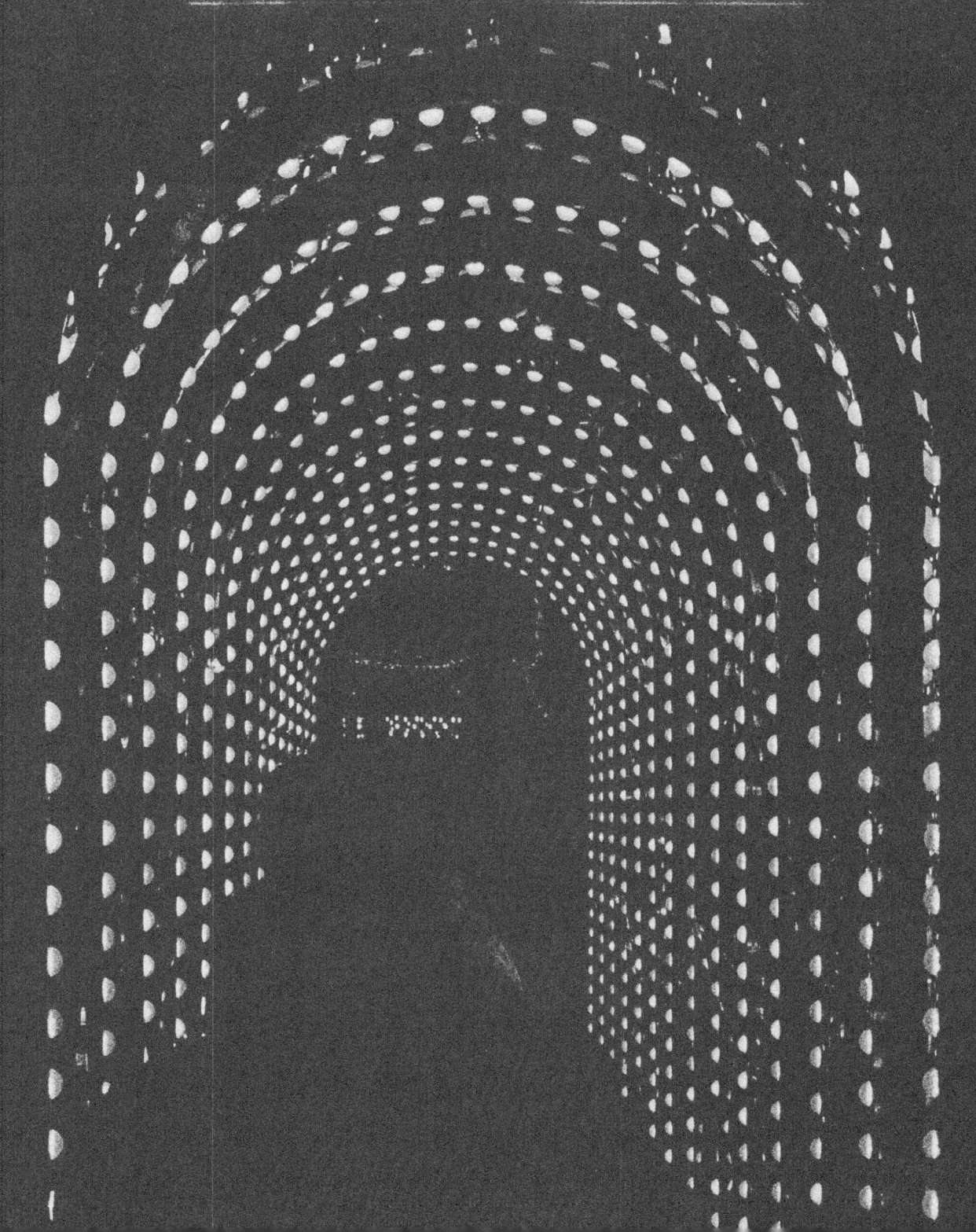

Have you ever made a promise to yourself to let something go? But not an hour later you pick it up again?

Why do we do that?? When I give myself the grace to put down something heavy, I continuously remind myself early on there is no need to carry that weight any more... and for the love of Mary not pick it up again.

How often do you ask for help?

There have been moments where things are falling apart and I am annoyed or angry where I often just think....let me do this myself. I have learned there is power in these few words 'I need your help.' Often the tension diffuses and you have a better shot of seeing eye to eye on the issue or with the person. Can't hurt to try it... especially when other things aren't working!

Find the Right Now Role

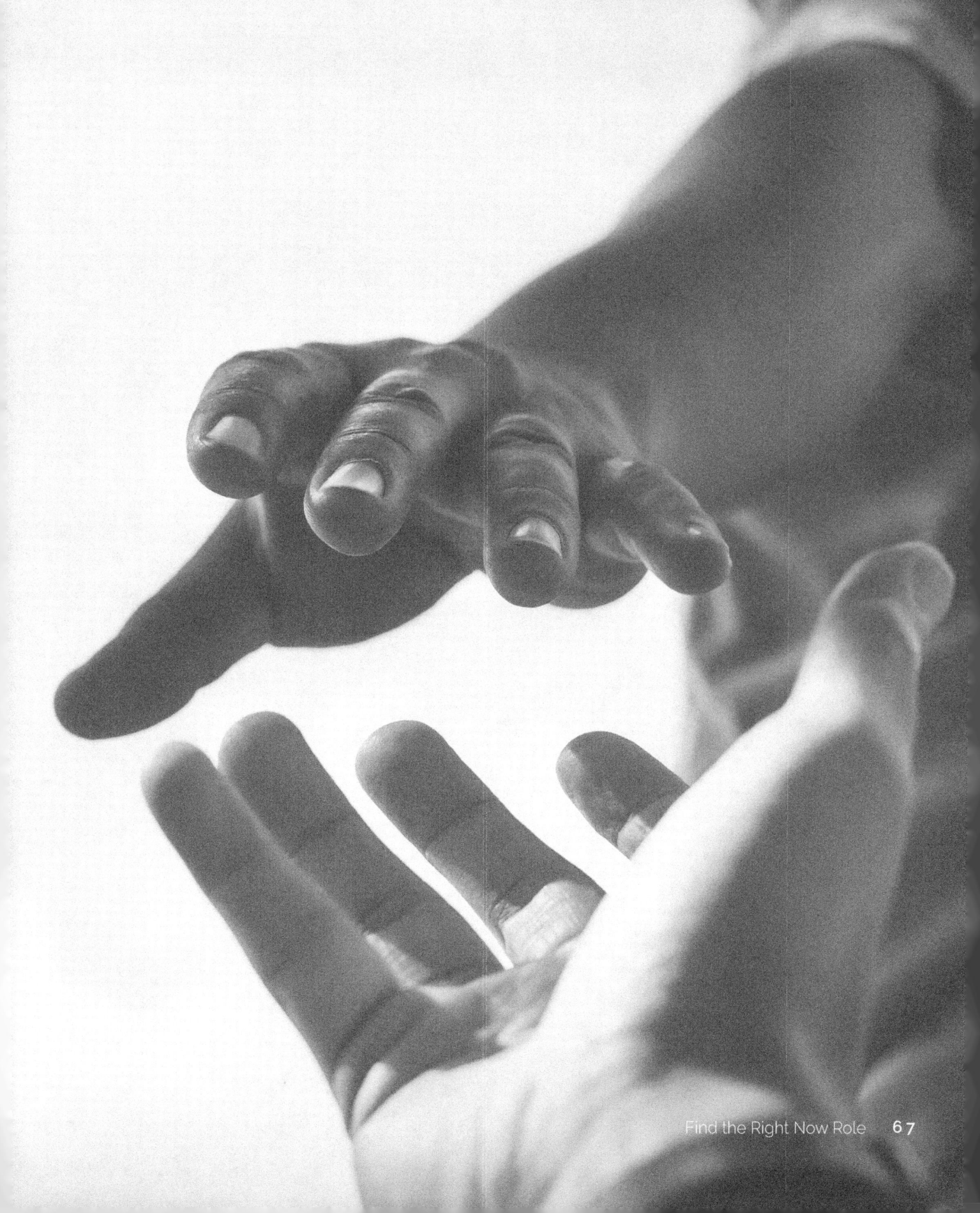

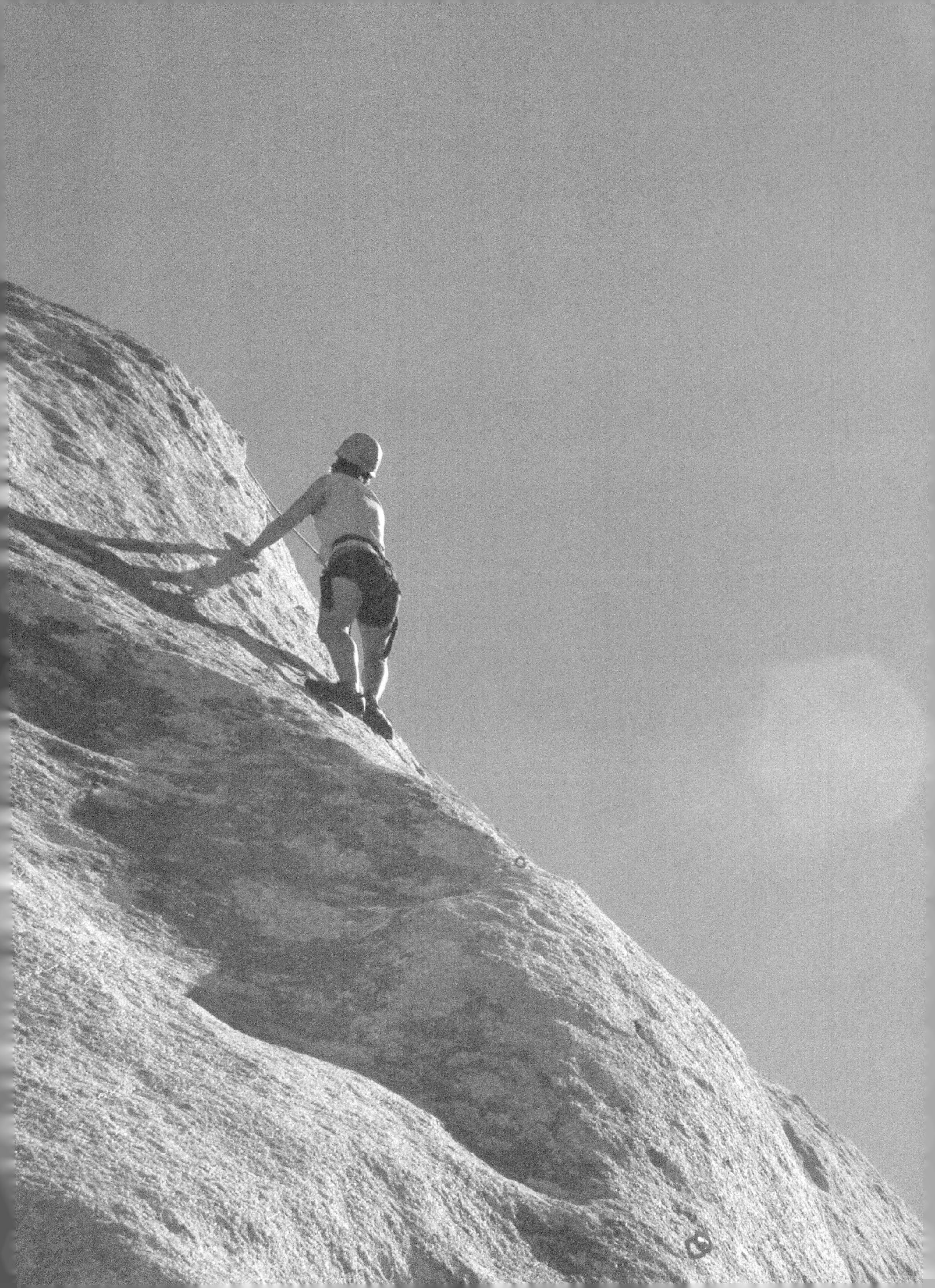

Start doing hard things... .. post on LinkedIn, write a blog, make the cold call. Challenge yourself everyday to do something new. If it isn't uncomfortable you aren't growing. And yes, no one says growing and learning is fun everyday, but once you learn something new and have a new skill keep at it... .. you'll be surprised how in time you will be great at it!

Like looking for a partner or spouse... that company is out there looking for you. It is just a matter of time until you find each other. There may be companies that aren't ready for you yet or may not have an opening - talk with them anyway. A key part of networking is making sure people know you are 'out there'.

Find the Right Now Role

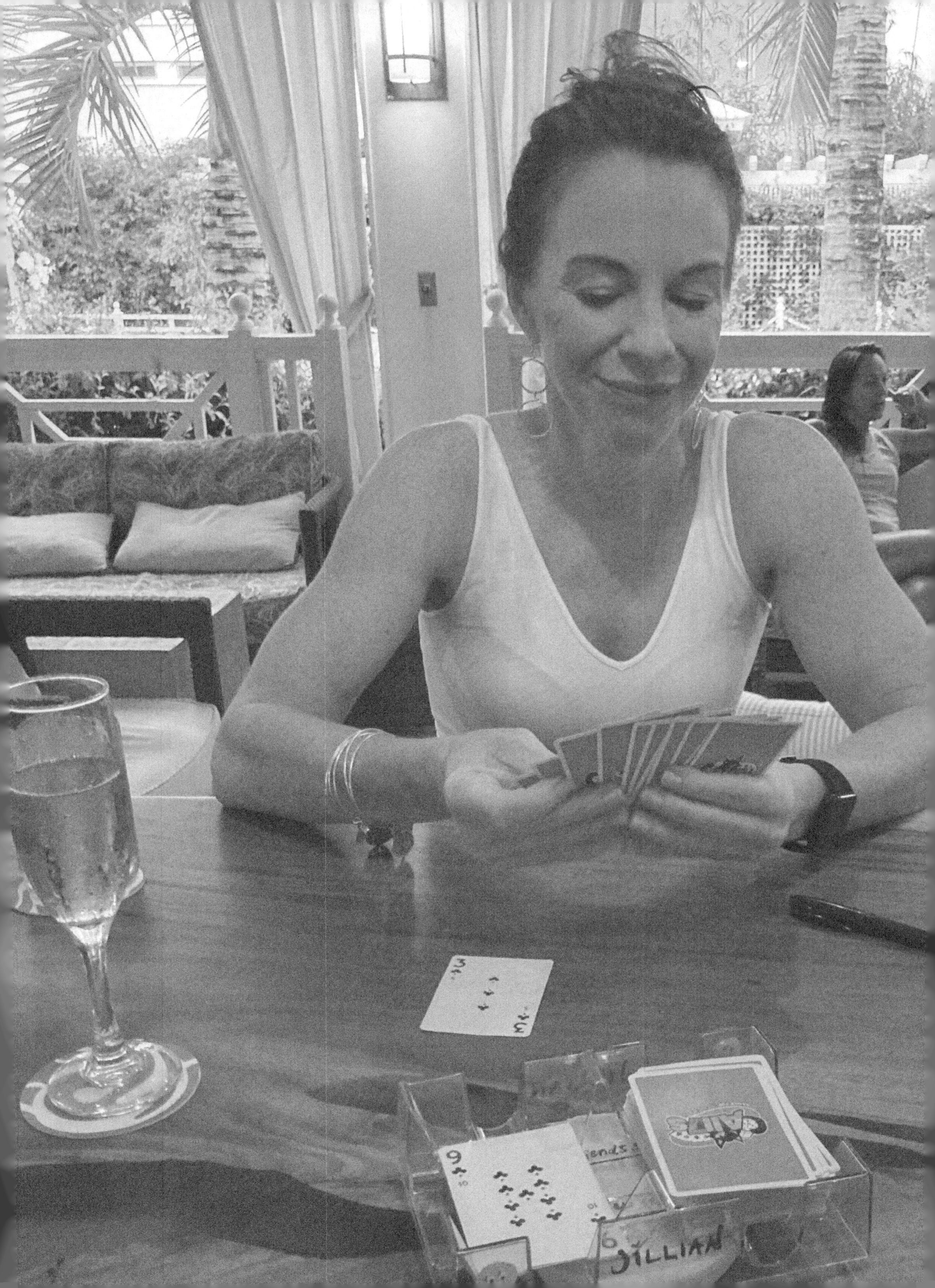
JILLIAN

Your dream job is 100% possible.... The stories you tell yourself and the beliefs you have will create the next phase of your life... so start telling yourself the story about what your new job 'looks' and 'feels' like... .that way when it shows up... you know it when you see it.

Like that card you need for a clean canasta....
right ladies?!?

Find the Right Now Role

Interviewing is practice... not permanent... and you will get so good at it you can do it in your sleep. Practice, practice, practice. In the beginning, it was helpful in every interview to 'practice' telling my story, which examples I would give and why.

Lucky for Jack he doesn't need much practice at his golf game (unlike his mother).

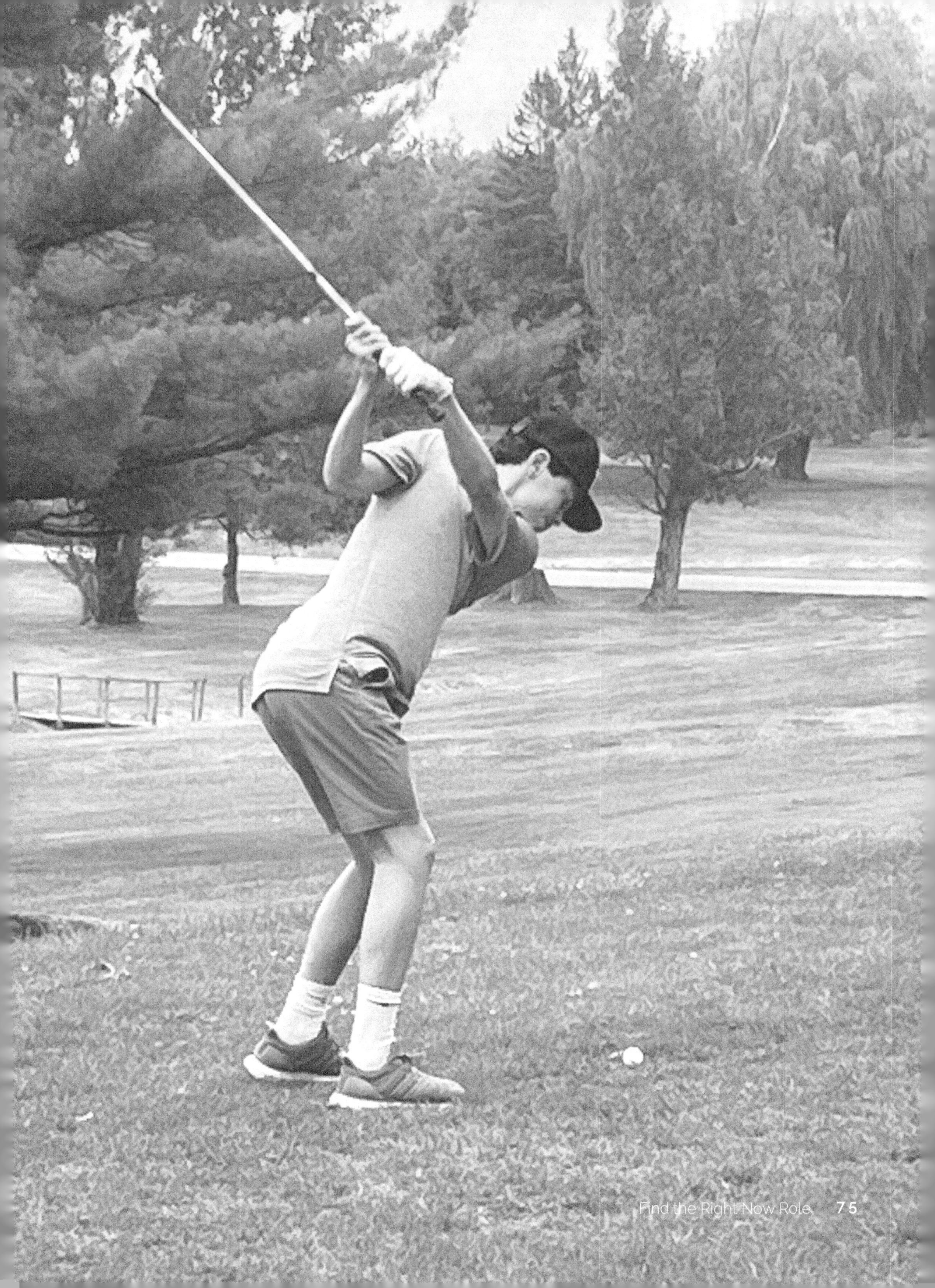

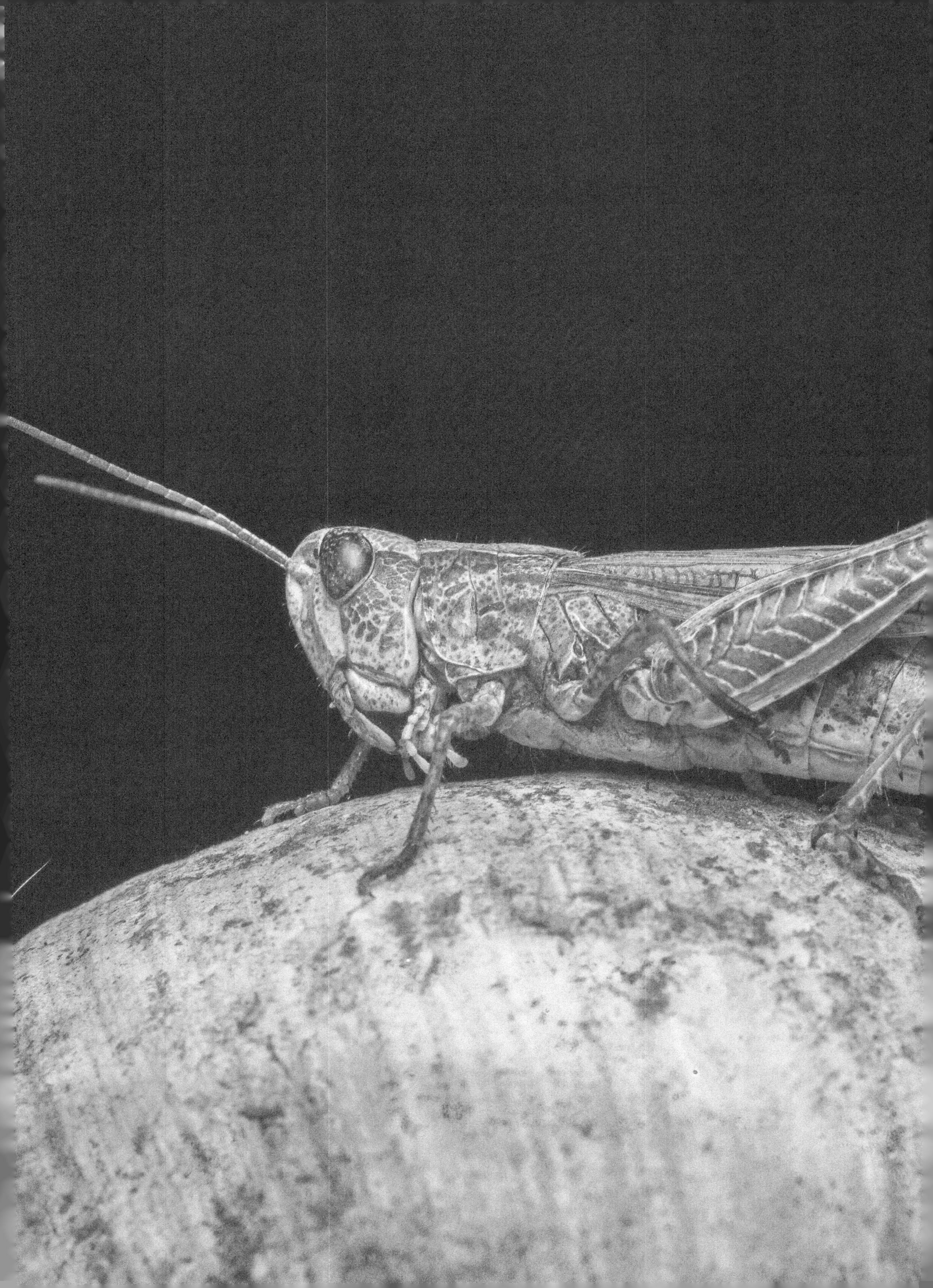

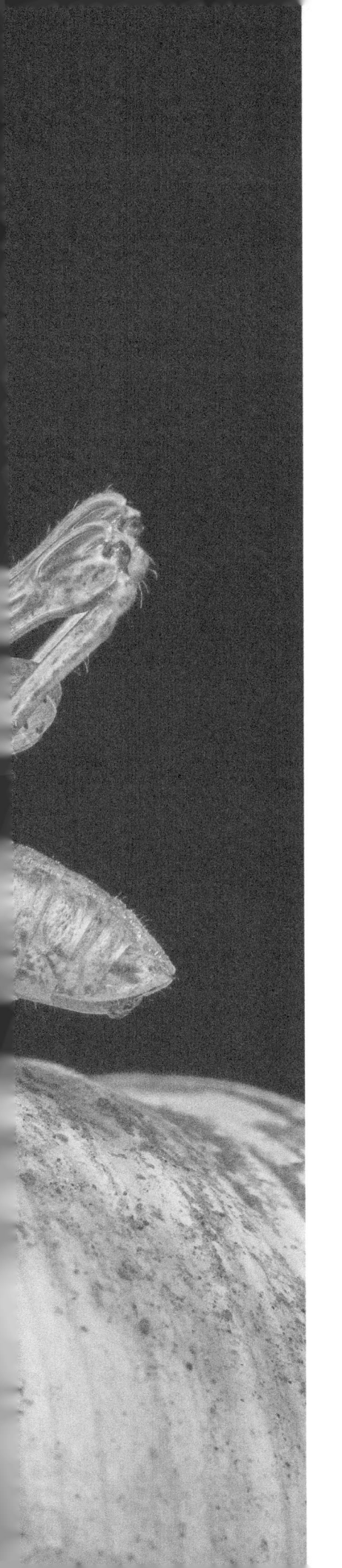

You are going to screw up... as in 'Those words didn't come out right.' Or 'I blanked on the answer to a question and there were crickets.' Remember - It. Is. All. Ok.   It is about the process, learning new skills and doing hard things. You will come out the other side tougher, stronger and more confident in how to think on your feet.

Explore 'in the meantime' opportunities... can you volunteer as an industry speaker or consult part-time or even write a book! One of the best parts of my process was part time consulting that enabled me to keep my mind fresh, gain a window into other companies, explore technology solutions that were new to me and create income. Also, gave me something interesting to talk about in interviews!

Find the Right Now Role 79

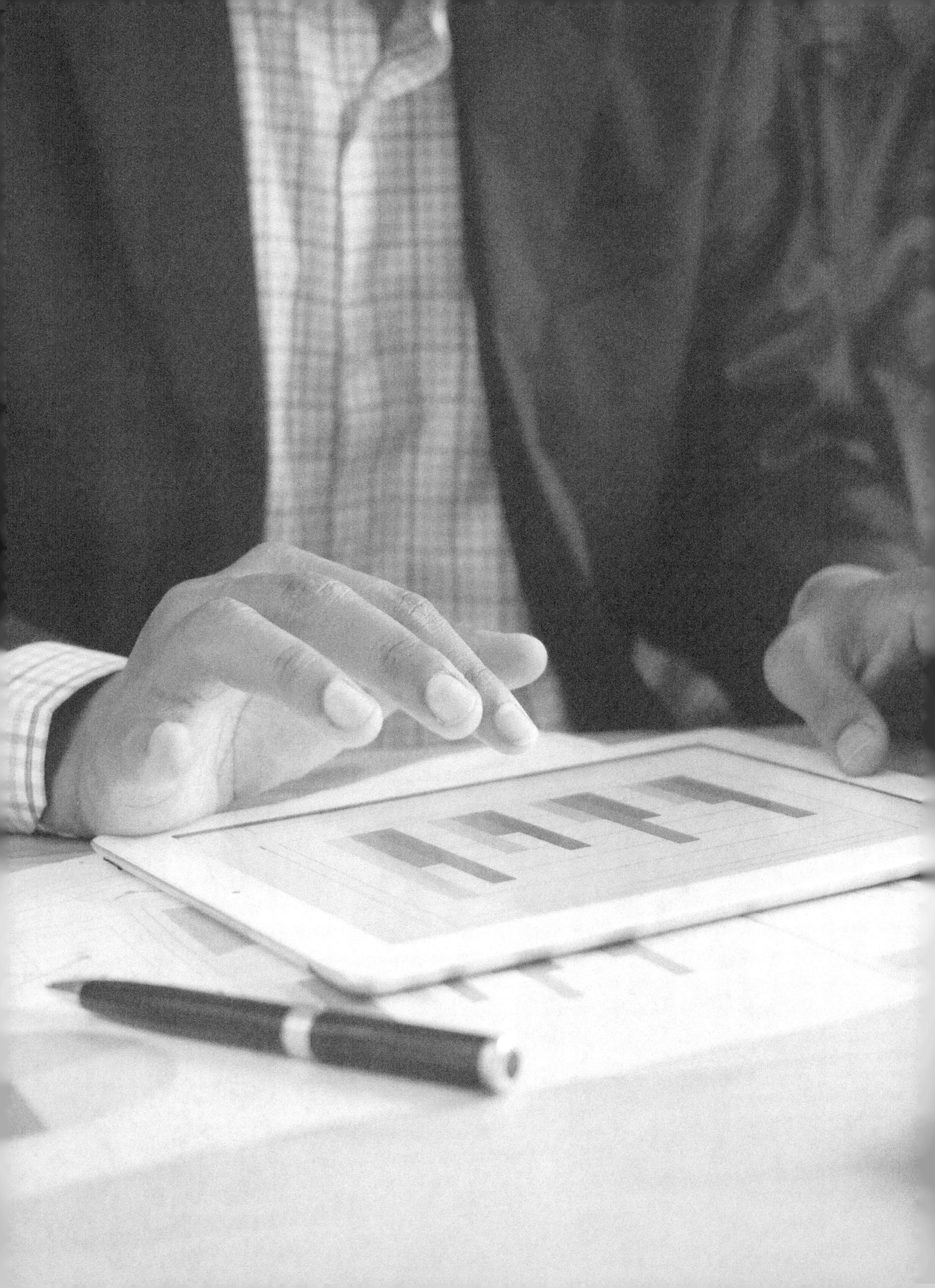

Spend time on your finances (again)... review where you are with your financial planner. This is a great way to validate your timeline to get through to the next role... reinforcing the 'side hustle' idea!

You can over do it. While at first I raced out of the gate to fill 8+ hours a day with networking meetings, you need to make time for self-care. Find activities that recharge your energy and make the time to do them. This is a marathon not a sprint.

GREAT CIRCLE

was a worse mess than th
nelling of decay. A
e table. Jan

Find the Right Now Role 83

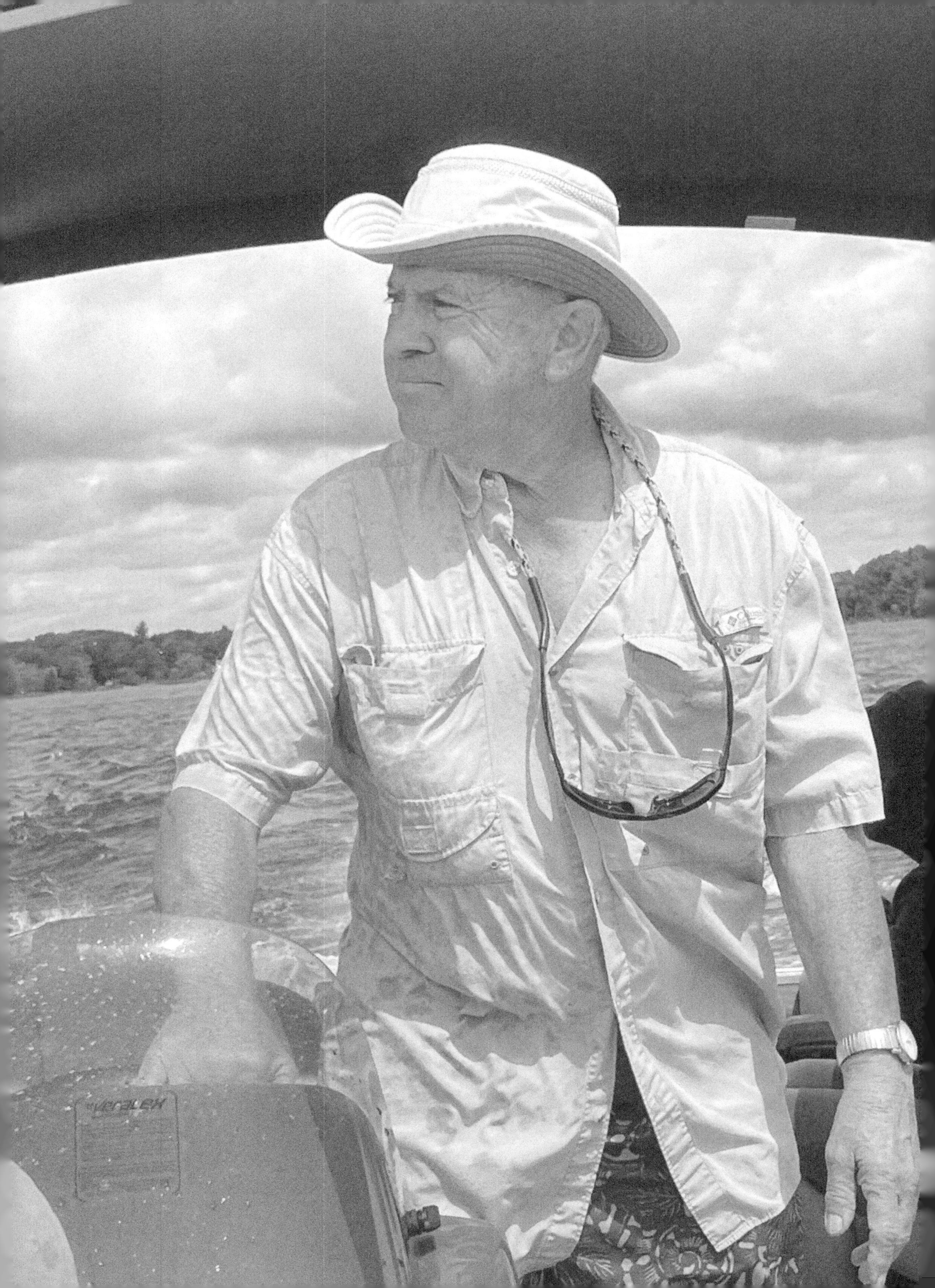

Plan your life... book the trip, make the plans, buy the tickets... don't wait til you find the job. The job will find you. Embrace that you can take that vacation without worrying about work, deliverables and email to clear.

This is Captain Tony... not a care in the world at the helm of a boat... be like Tony.

While I directionally may know where I am headed and how to get there, I have learned having the confidence and courage to try and having an idea and voicing it are more important than knowing 100% of the answer.

As the cowardly lion says, 'I am content in knowing I am as brave as any best that ever lived, if not braver.' Where will you be courageous today?

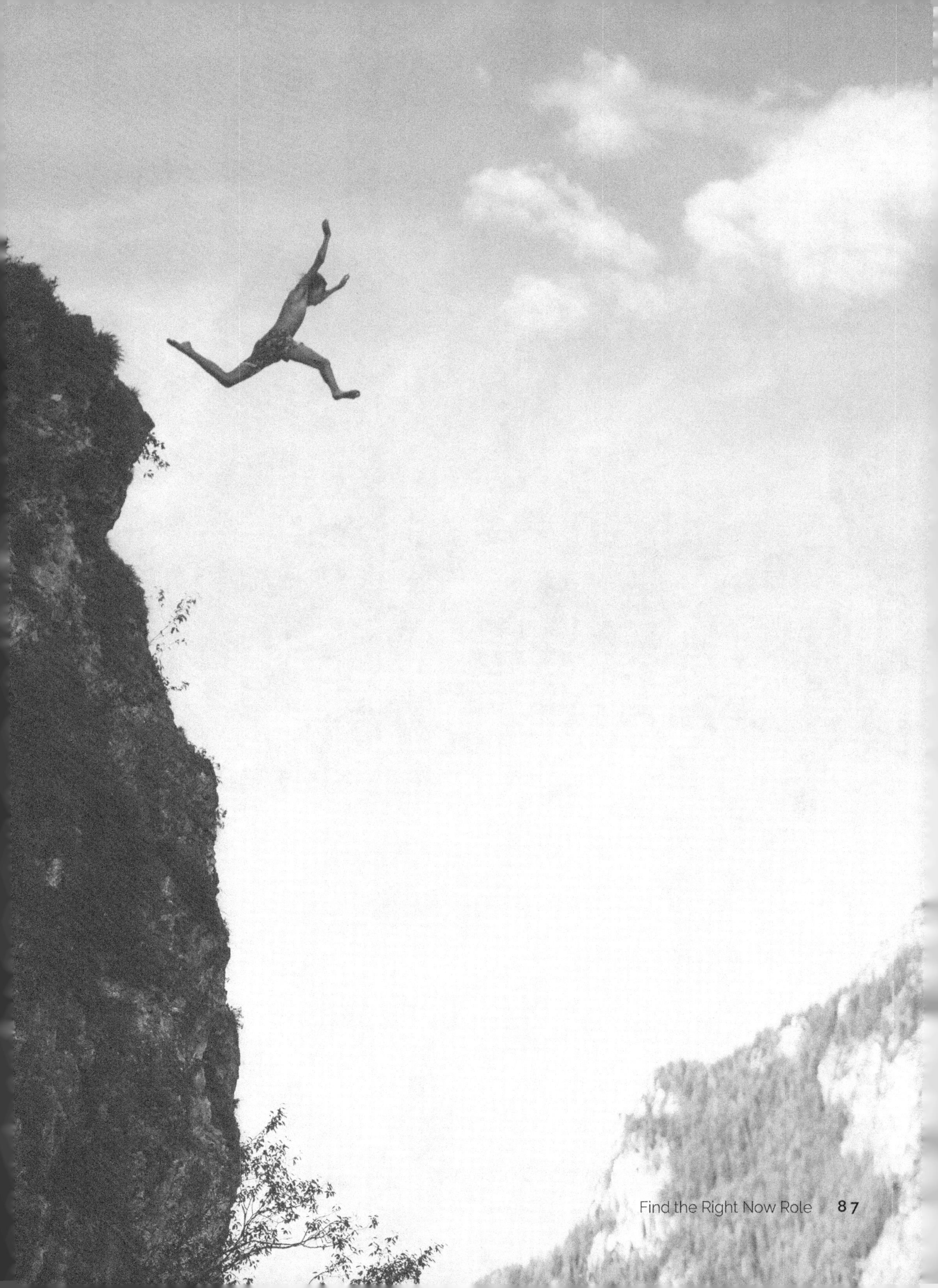

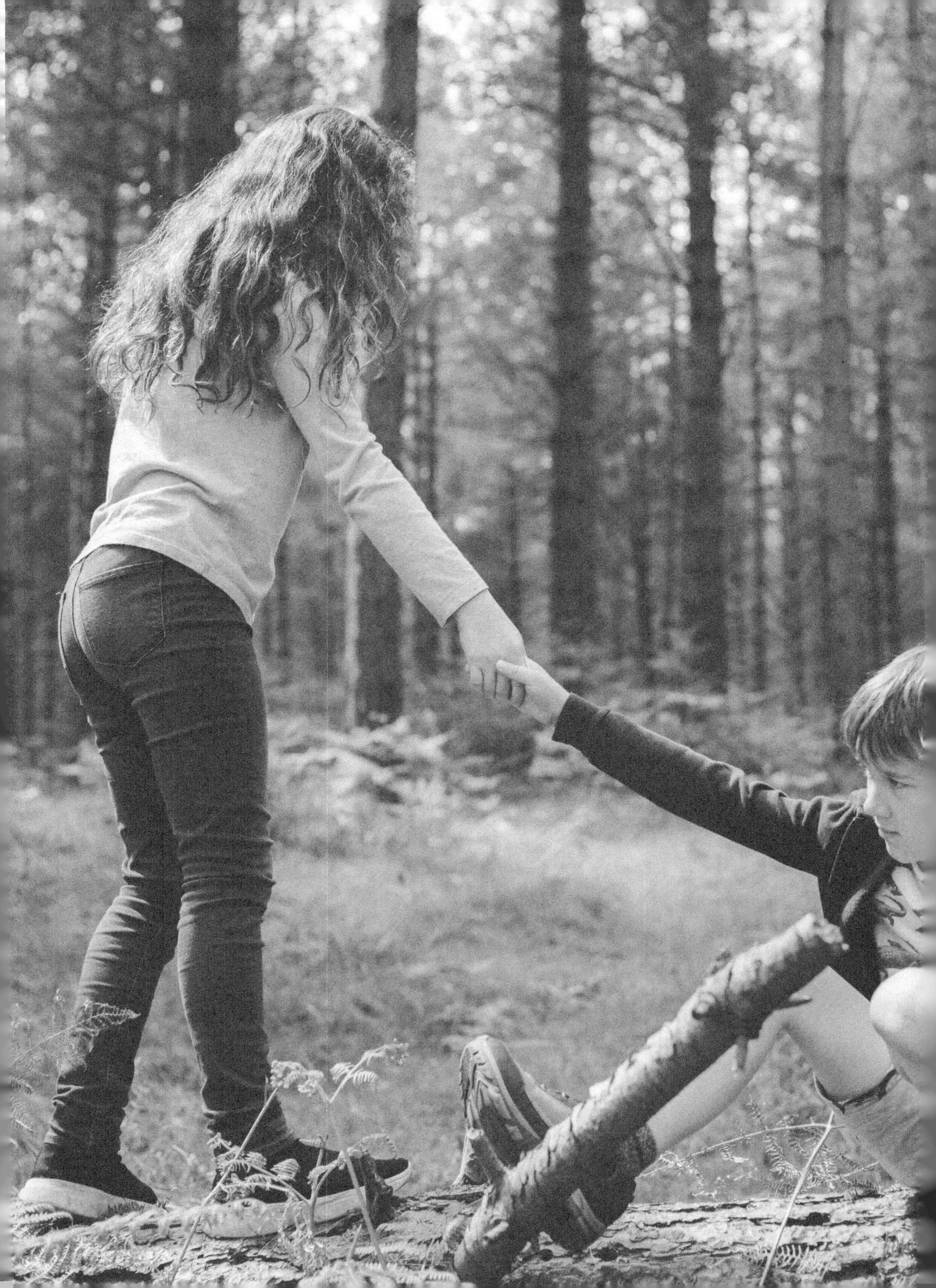

So have you asked for help today? I know you have a plan and an itinerary for what actions you need to take to land that job, but have you stepped back and asked for help. I practice this daily. It doesn't come easy for me. I often feel like I SHOULD have the answers on my own. But guess what, there are no medals for doing this (or anything for that matter) solo.

You need to be where you are to get where you are going. I remind myself daily to embrace the NOW... the now in my relationships and career journey... to be grateful for all I am learning and the excitement and joy that the NOW brings me. For the times that are challenging or trying, I remember to breathe and go slow. What if embracing the NOW got you to the next thing faster???

Find the Right Now Role

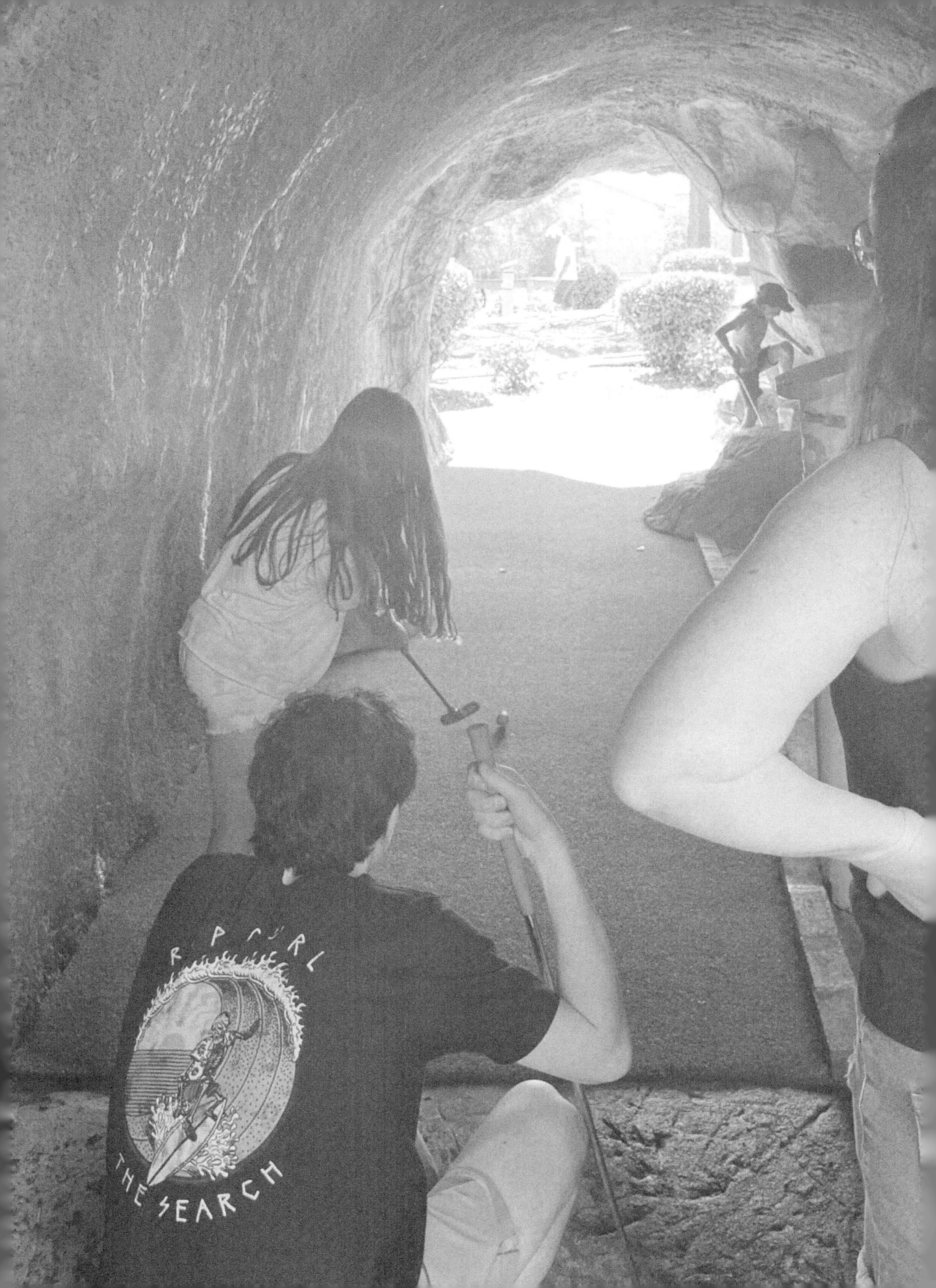
THE SEARCH

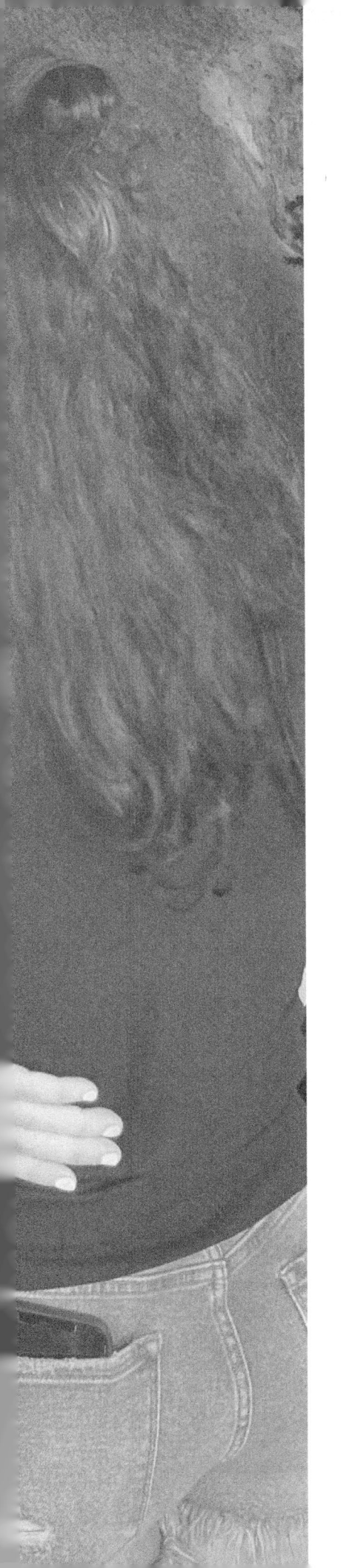

How do you set yourself up for a success or a challenge… It is the same. You step back and determine what your first next step is. You don't need to solve steps 1-100, just step 1. I am reminded of this when things are going well or when I feel like I am in quick sand. Or in this case line up the putt in mini golf.

It is ok to not be ok. Truly... you will have days when you just don't feel up to it, when you really aren't ok and it is fine... it is actually better than fine. And remember there were days in your last job where you weren't ok, or in your next job where you will not be ok. Totally normal... and yes you have permission to not think the world is rainbows and unicorns. In my family nothing cheers others up more than getting a face time from most of the clan.

Find the Right Now Role　95

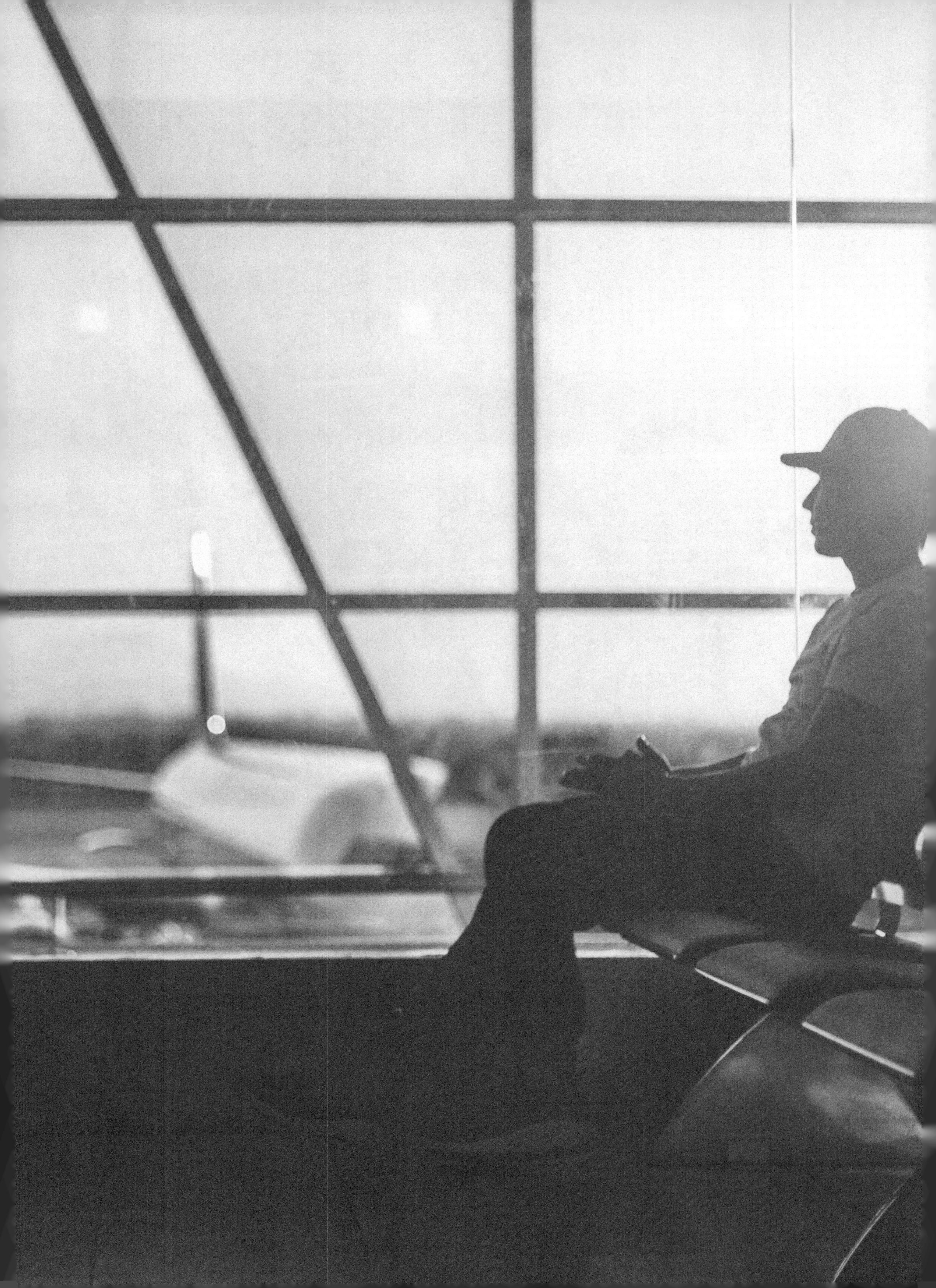

When was the last time you waited for something... truly wallowed in the joy of anticipation whether an event, vacation, job or relationship. In our era of instant gratification, I find it doesn't happen often. However, when it does it can be beautiful and nerve wracking all at the same time. This is a reminder to enjoy every stop and milestone along the way to get there... and don't bother crossing those fingers if it is for you it will come to you.

What if it was happening for you instead of to you? Those challenges, obstacles, hard discussions and things to solve for… what if they were opening the door for you to be able to do more, be more… and allow you to be more at ease and comfortable. I continue to be reminded the challenges will come, but my experience has taught me 'how' to respond and react… and even while I am working through the 'it', my muscle memory says 'you have seen this before', 'not your first rodeo', 'you got this'!

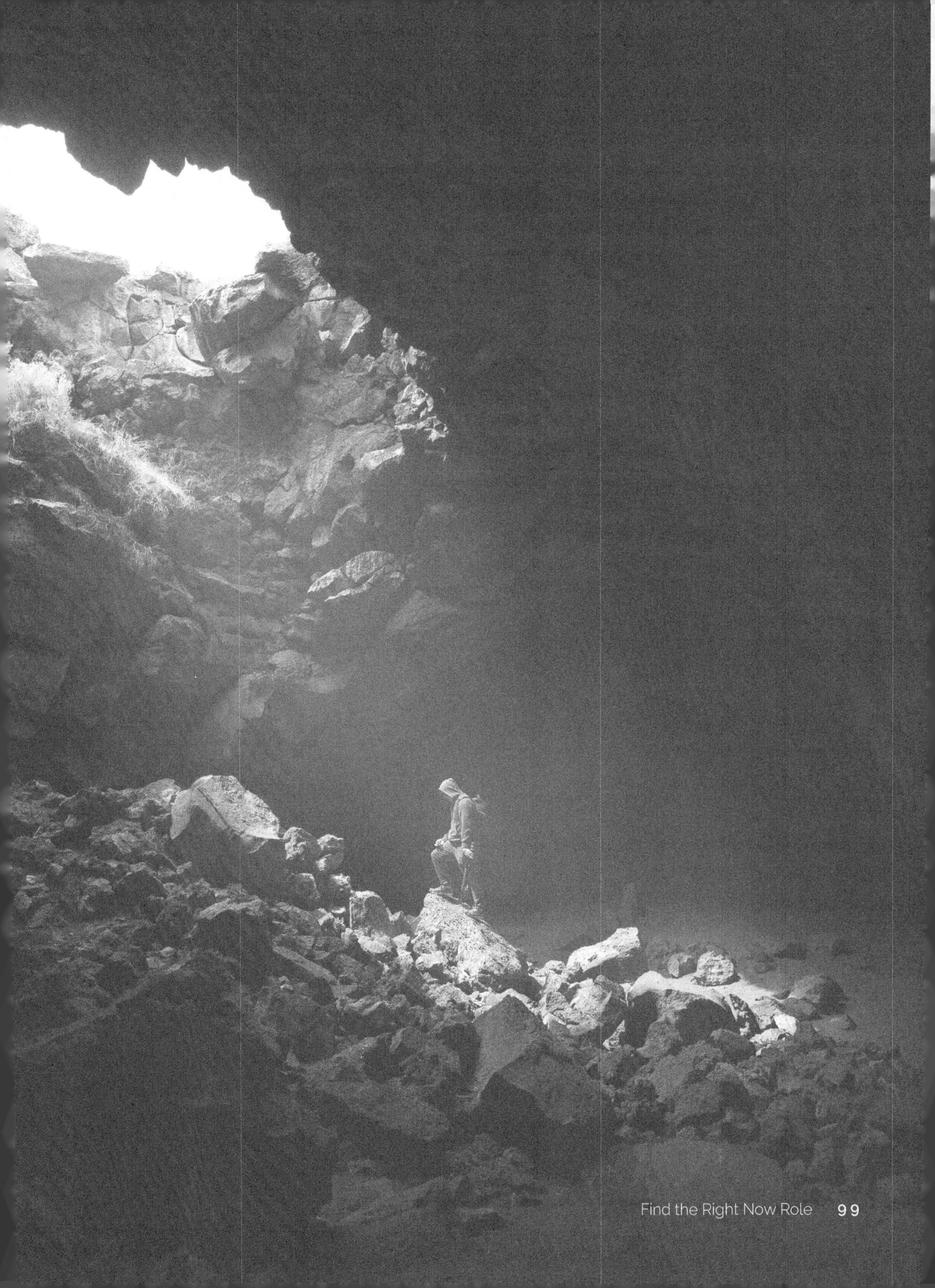

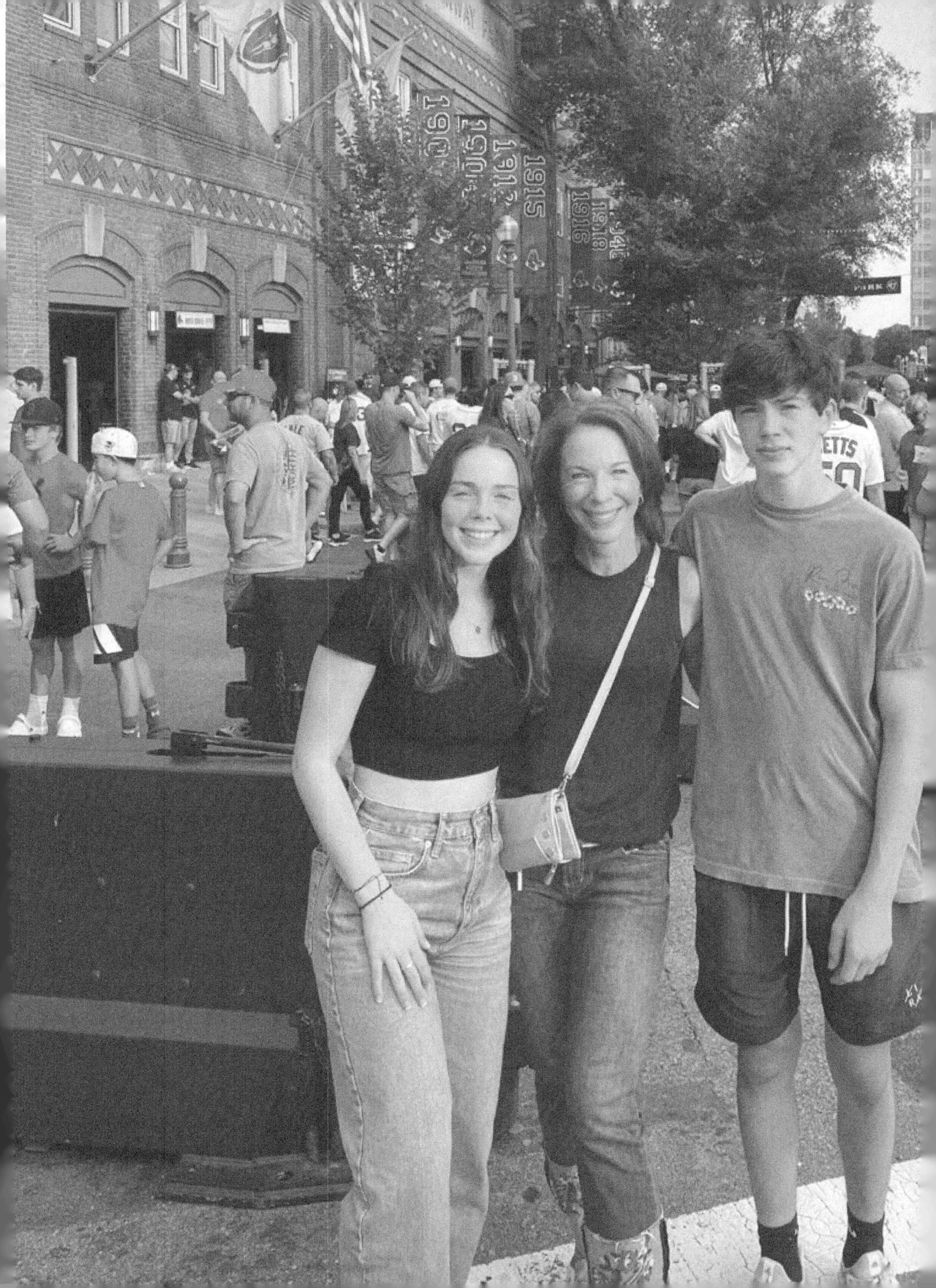
1915
1916
1918

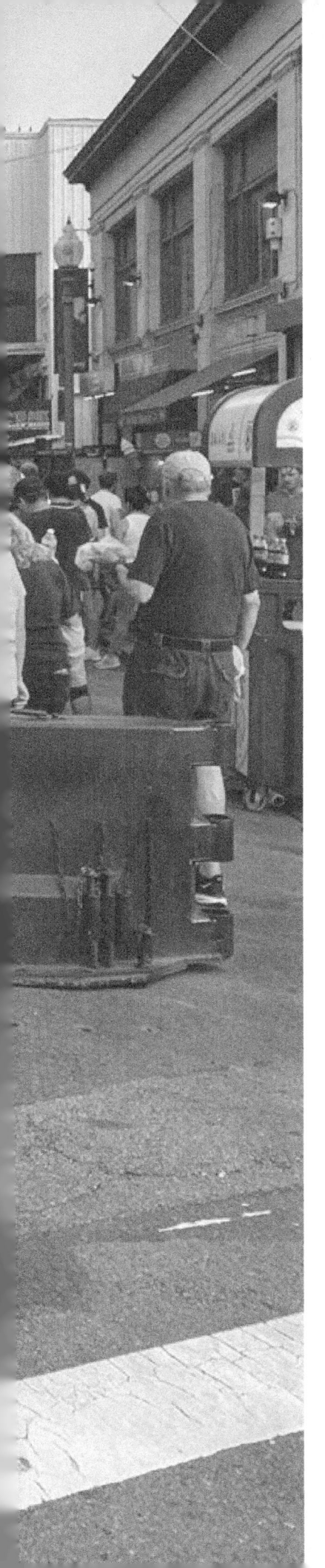

When plan A fails move to plan B and make it the best you got!

My summer vacation plans with the kids were rearranged this week by Covid but we still had an awesome week.

Reminds me that when things don't go according to plan personally or professionally you can dwell in it (which I did for a moment) and then you can move on. Thankful for showing my kids the power of the pivot!

Has it ever not gone your way? Or was the outcome not what you had hoped for? Luckily I have had plenty of practice... I have learned in these moments to look for the lesson, see the opportunity and know better things are coming. And in the most recent words of my daughter... we just keep moving forward!

Find the Right Now Role   103

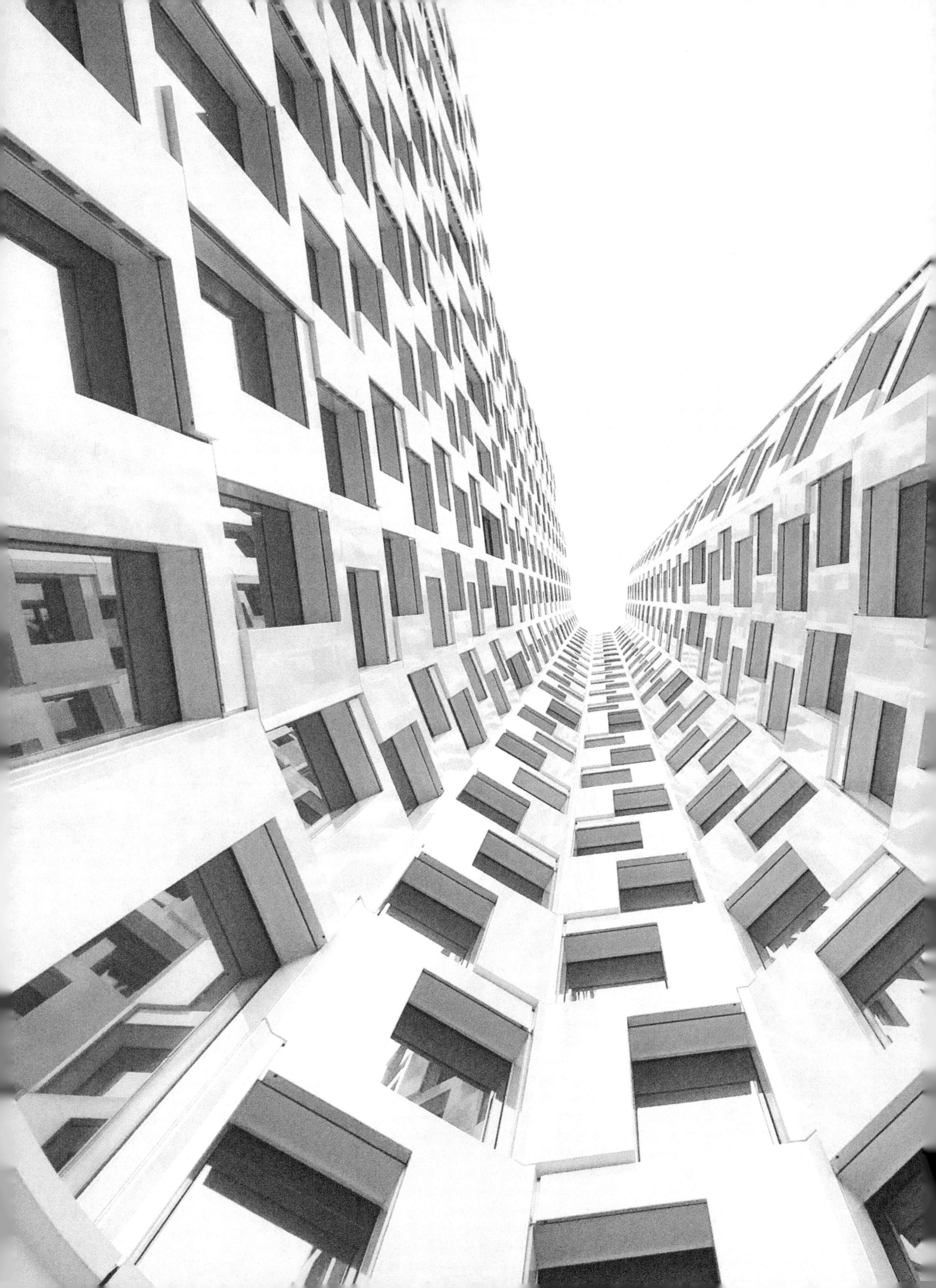

What do you do when you feel stuck? For me, I back up... I pull my brain out of the weeds and look for a fresh perspective. And most importantly... I just stop doing and trying and pushing my way through. While I often say 'the only way through is through', often just being still is the best action to ensure forward progress.

My mom used to say, be careful what you wish for! The day had finally come... the day I had dreamed of and now I had multiple companies who had moved me to the final interview stage. Spend time to get really clear on what is important to you. How do you 'feel' in discussions w/ the leadership teams? What actions does each company take during the 'courting' process? For me this was a game changer, I evaluated the 'how' of the process just as much as the 'what' I was searching for.

Sort of like wishing for this day to come... .
Drive safe Jordan!

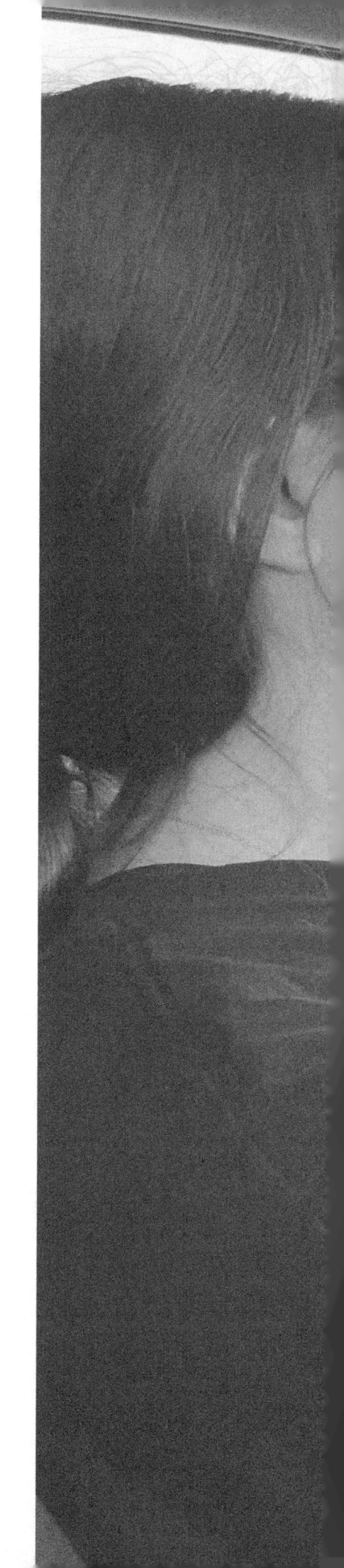

Find the Right Now Role

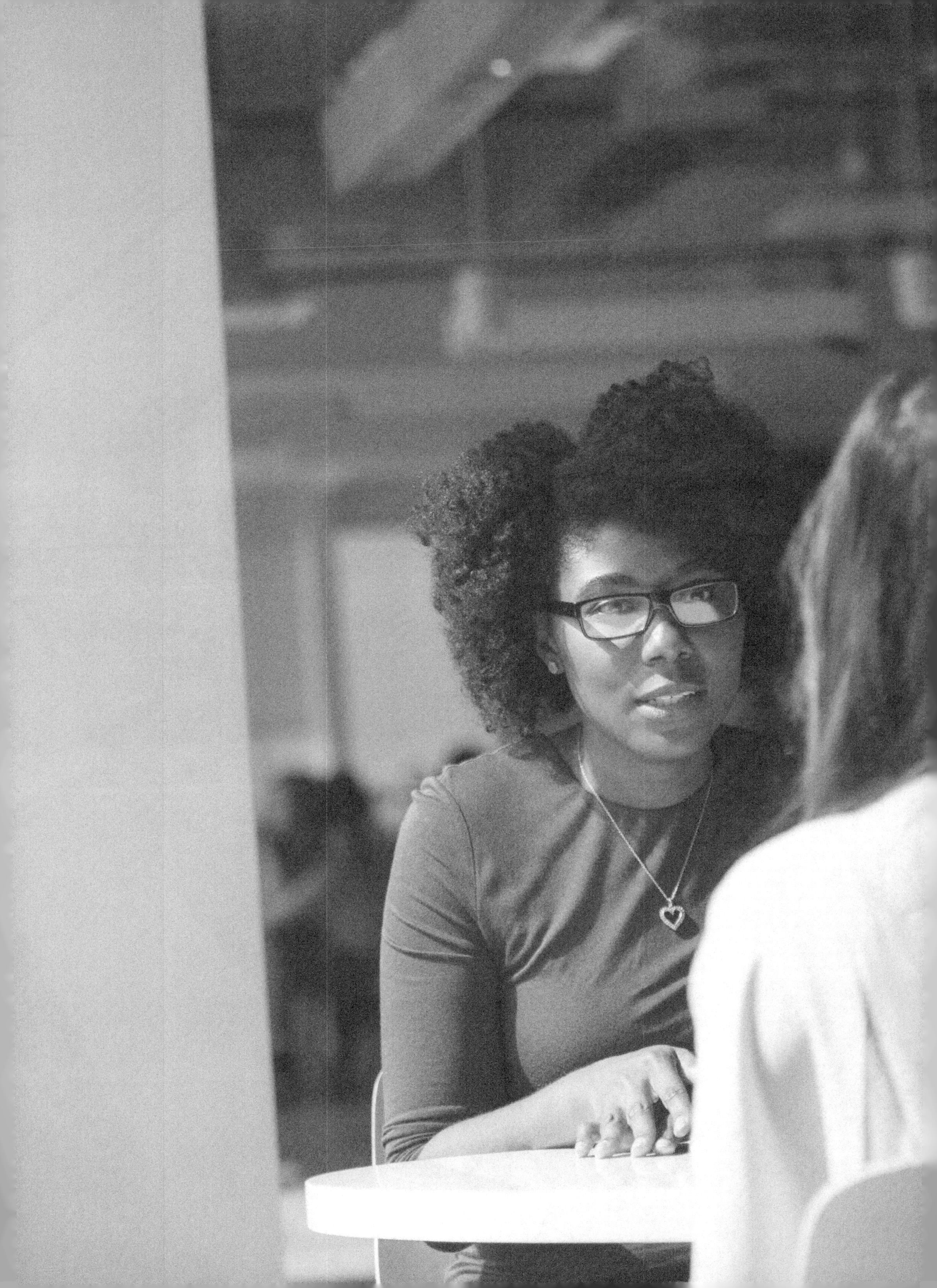

You need to interview them just as much as they interview you... .ask to meet with more people, talk with potential colleagues, customers and partners... make sure you have validated your assumptions by doing the work to align what they are offering you and what is important to you.

Be transparent... say it like it is and be direct, ask for the time you need to think about an offer, be honest about other opportunities you are evaluating. Leading with your authentic self from the start is important. Be who you say you are in the process.

This kind of transparency though... time for new sneakers. (Will protect the innocent for this one.)

Find the Right Now Role 111

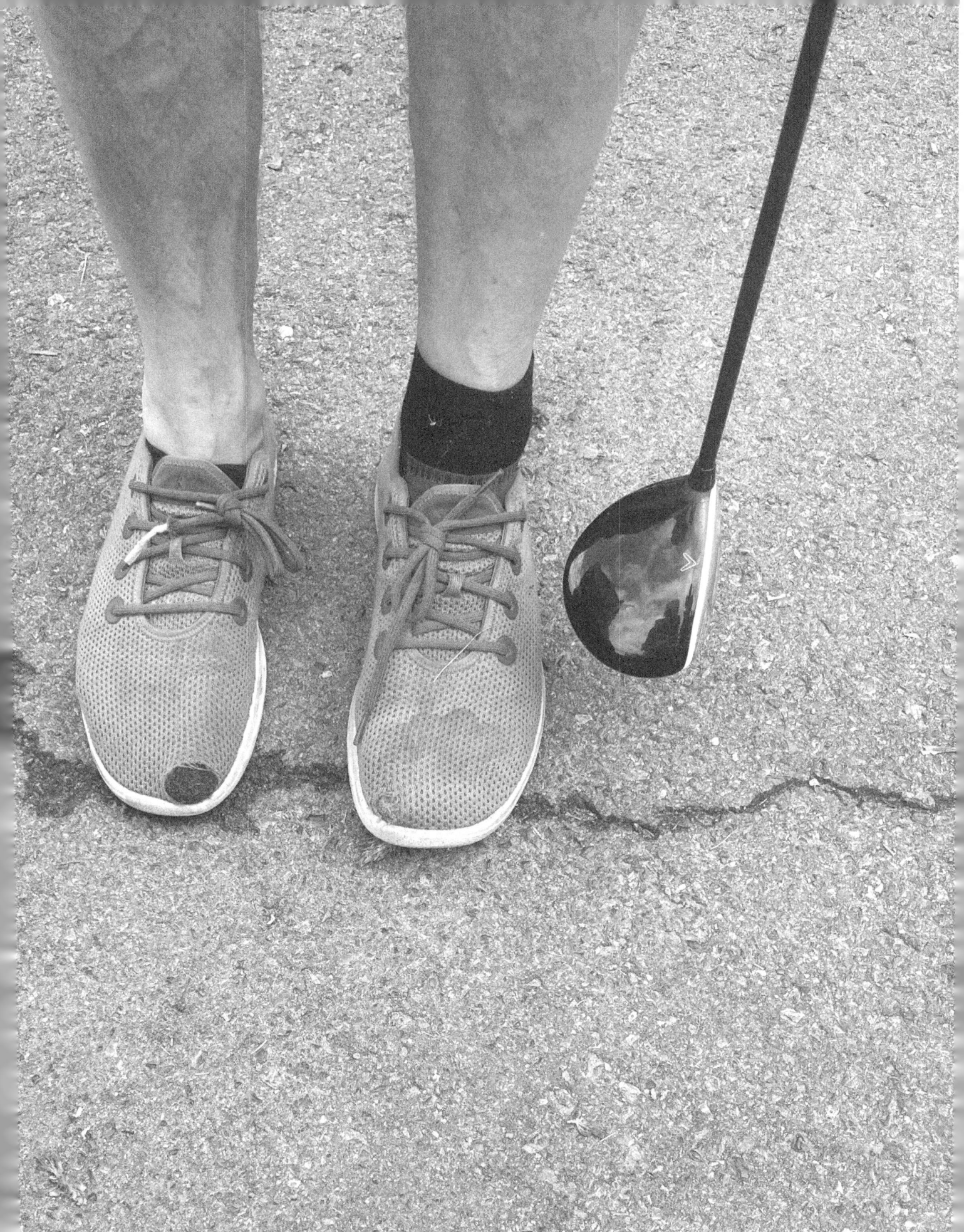

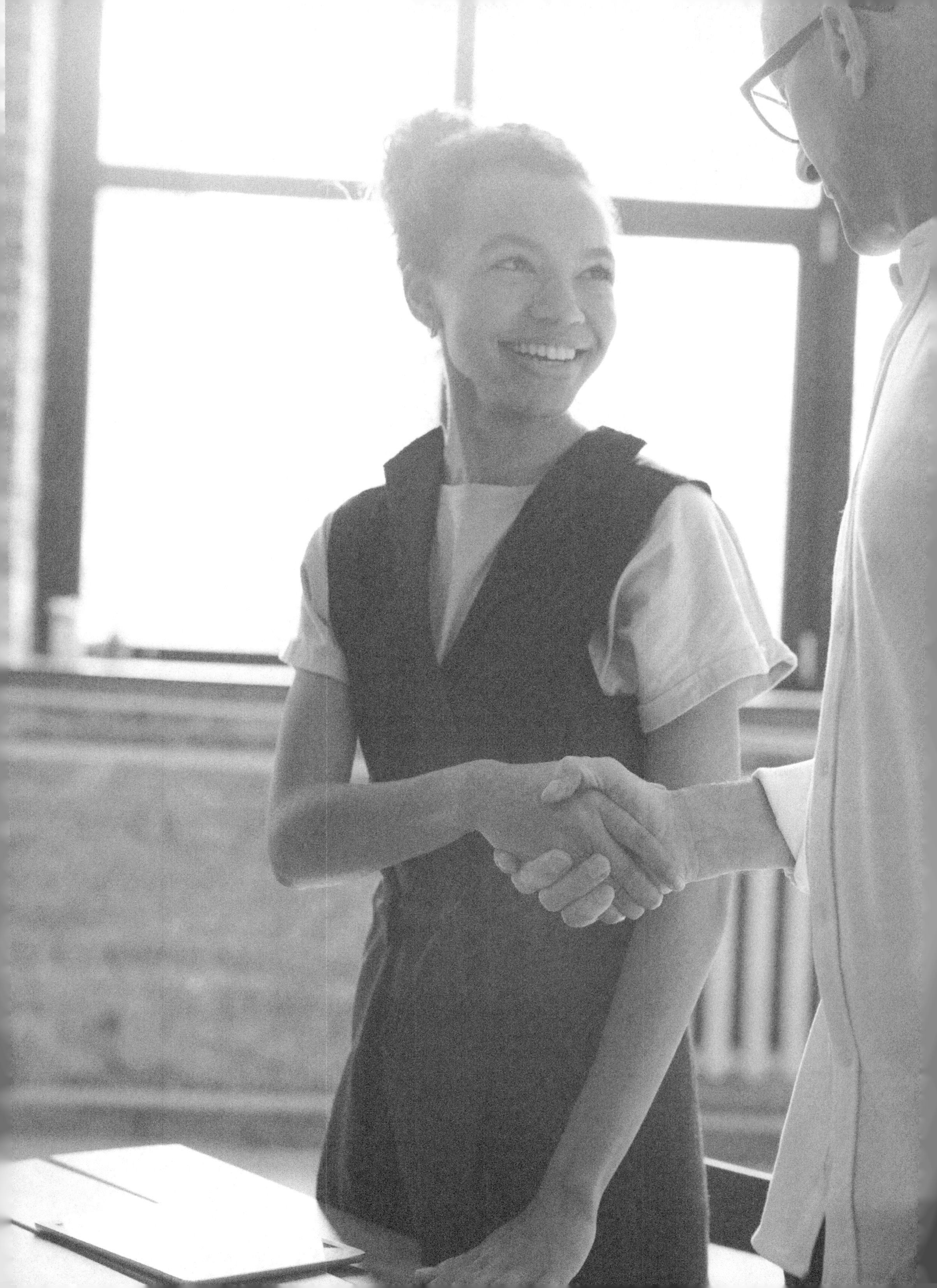

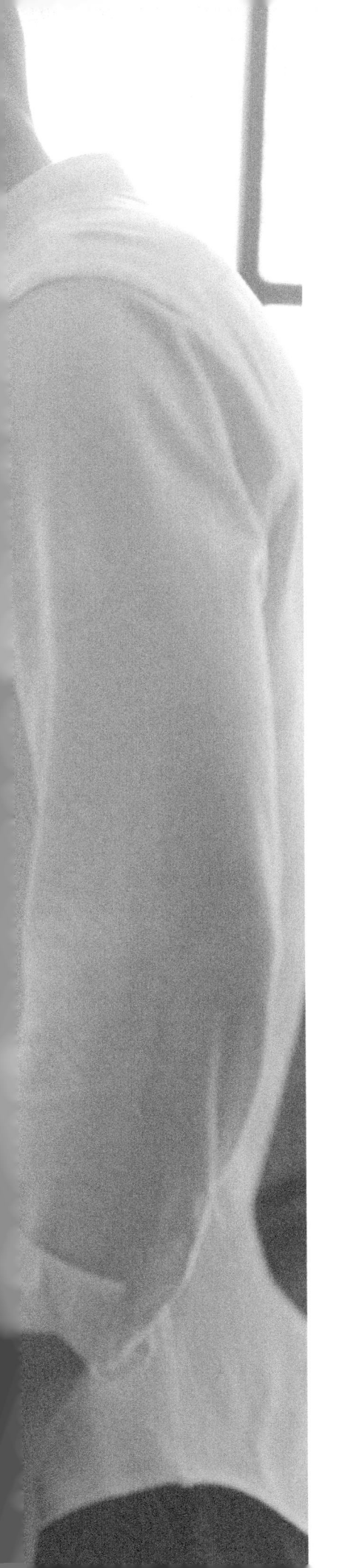

Negotiate... the right company, the right leadership team and the right role WILL meet you. Even if it is hard or uncomfortable....this is where coaches help... find people who want to protect your best interests and listen to their counsel.

Listen to your heart... while I have historically led
with my head in most professional decisions,
I focused more on listening to my heart and leaned
into understanding what environment
I would thrive in. When your heart is in it,
you will gladly give it your all without
even thinking about it.

When I am caught up in a song... my heart knows
I am where I belong.

Find the Right Now Role 115

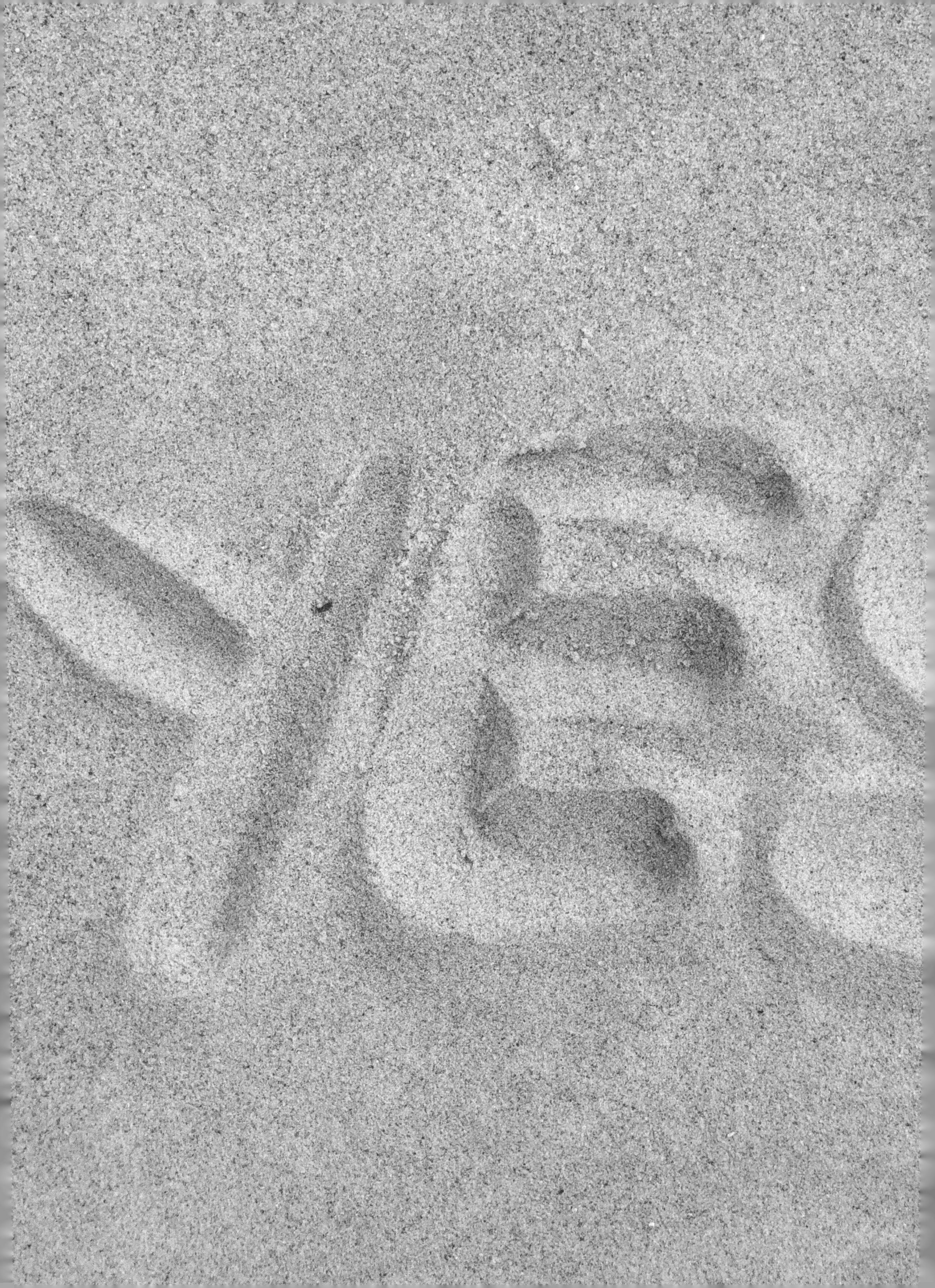

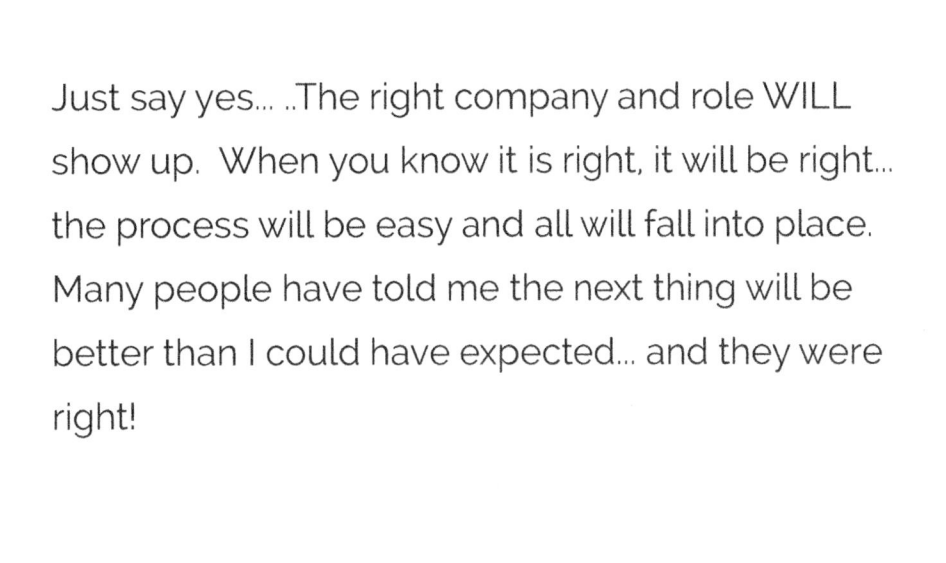

Just say yes... ..The right company and role WILL show up. When you know it is right, it will be right... the process will be easy and all will fall into place. Many people have told me the next thing will be better than I could have expected... and they were right!

Be patient....don't push it or rush through the process. I know the feeling... you are so close and you just want to move to your first day. The devil is in the details....get input from your advisors along the way. Remember how far you have come and reflect on your progress. The finish line is in sight!

Find the Right Now Role   119

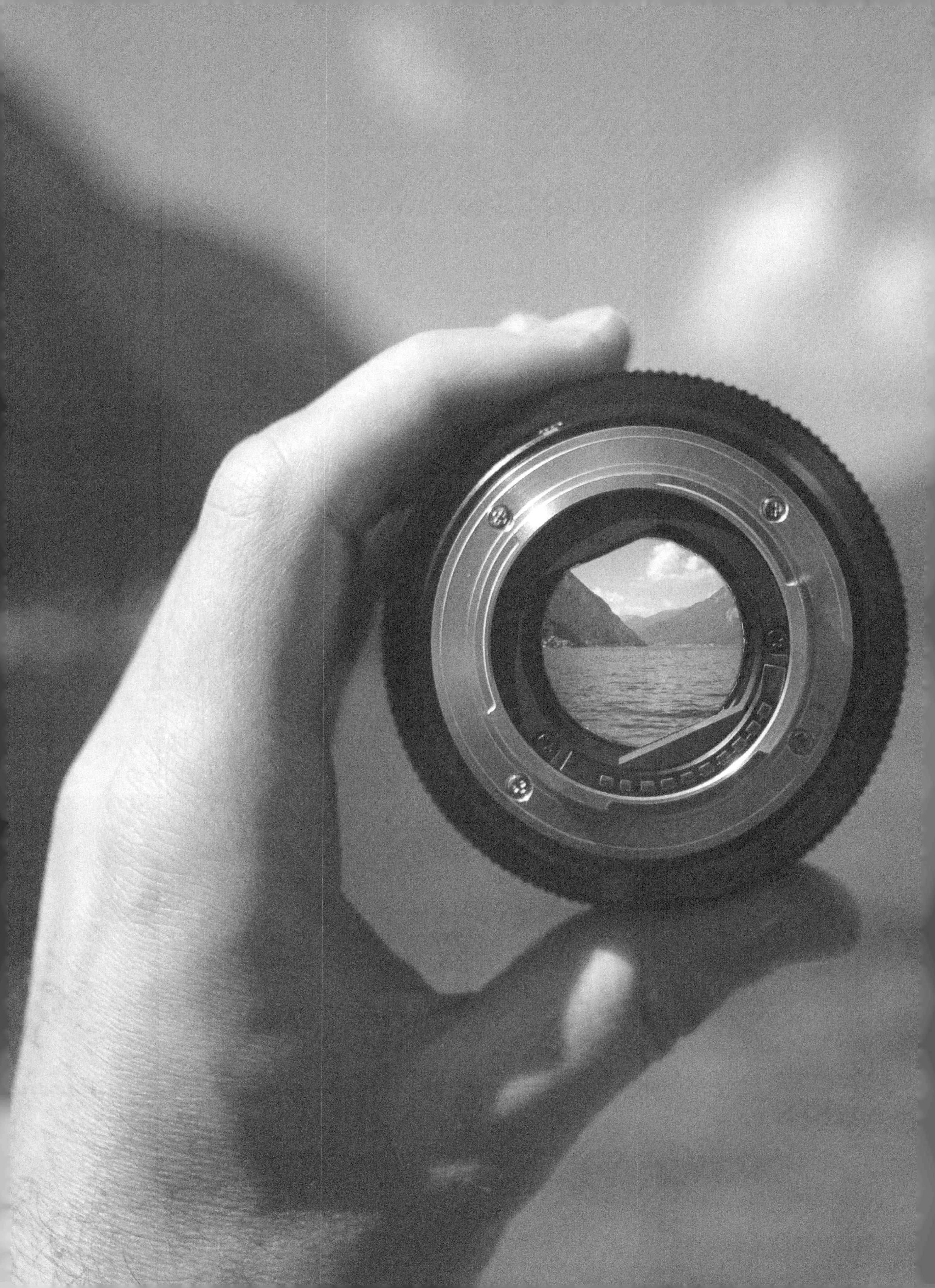

Narrow your focus... be honest with yourself on what opportunities are truly a match for you. If it doesn't feel like a fit, don't talk yourself into it. And don't worry about the job offer... until you get one.

What does close feel like to you?
For me, sometimes it is exhilarating, sometimes I am frustrated and sometimes I can be patient enough to enjoy the journey. I have learned that I can experience all these feelings as I work towards something... and it is all part of the process. Like being so close to that pin for my son... happy to report he got it!

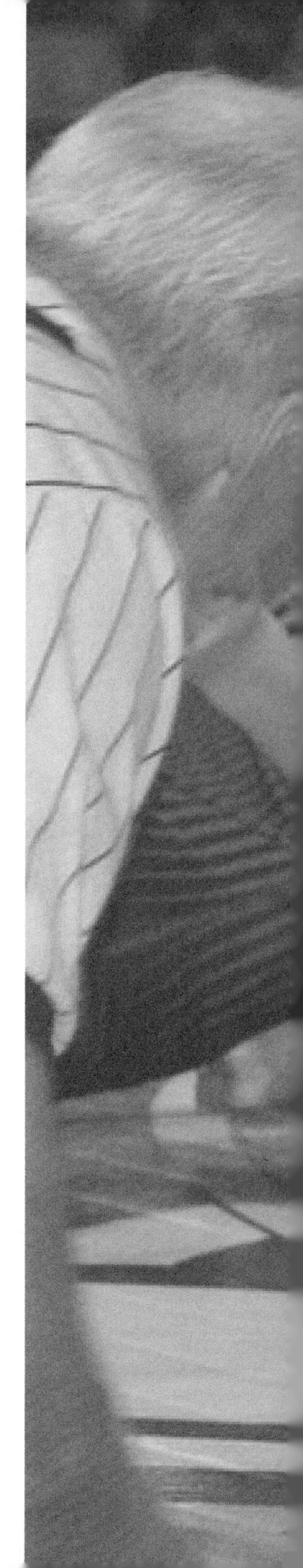

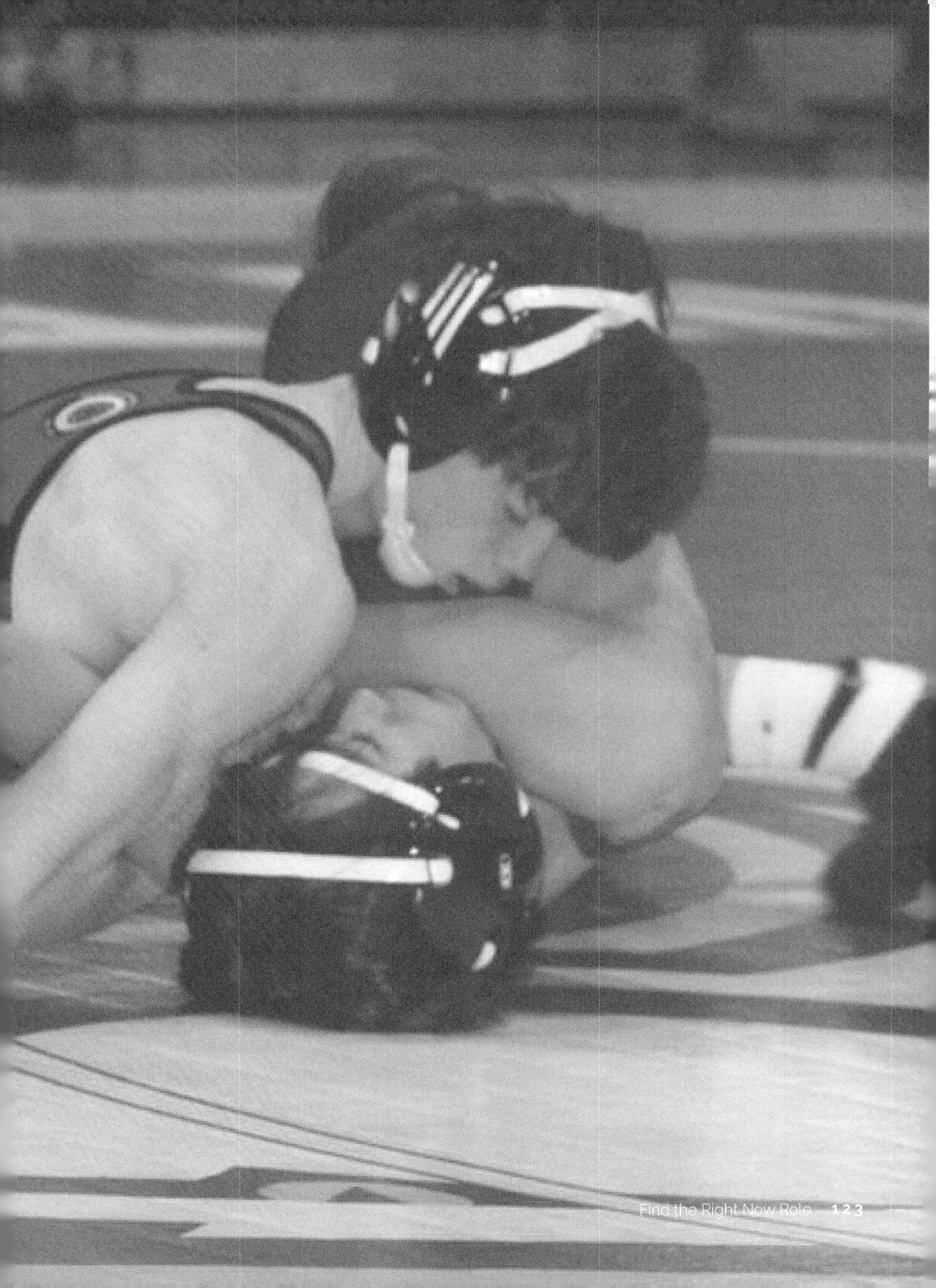

believe in

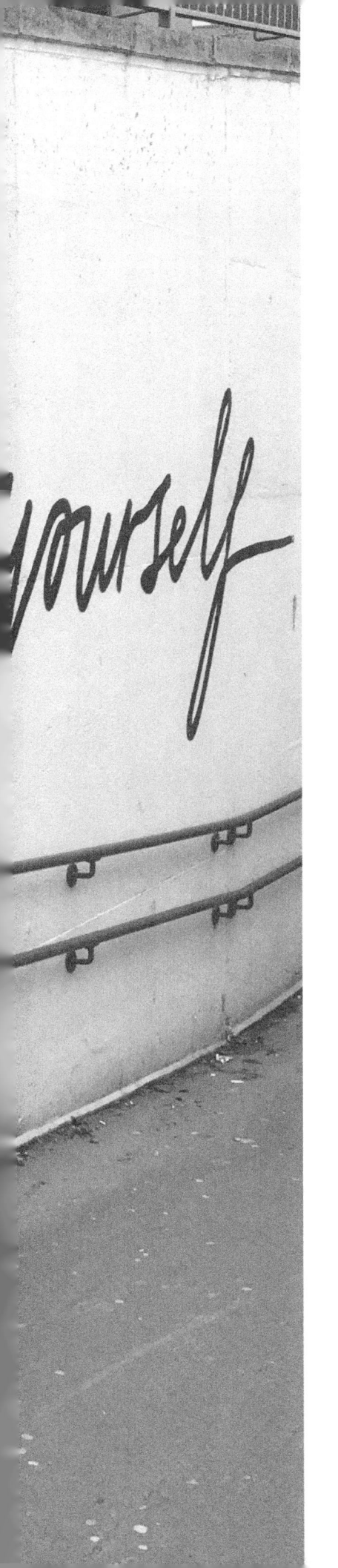

Your attitude determines your direction. How are you approaching your decision and options? Are you open minded? Are you asking the questions you need to understand more about your future role? How do those answers 'feel' to you? This is a critical time to stay positive and BELIEVE the right role will find you.

Are you always looking for the light, looking for the glimmer? Sunflowers do. I had the pleasure of spending this past weekend seeing all the good and light around me. I have learned that when you look for the good, look for the positivity and promise... at some point you find it... and it shines brighter than ever.
Be the sunflower!

Find the Right Now Role 127

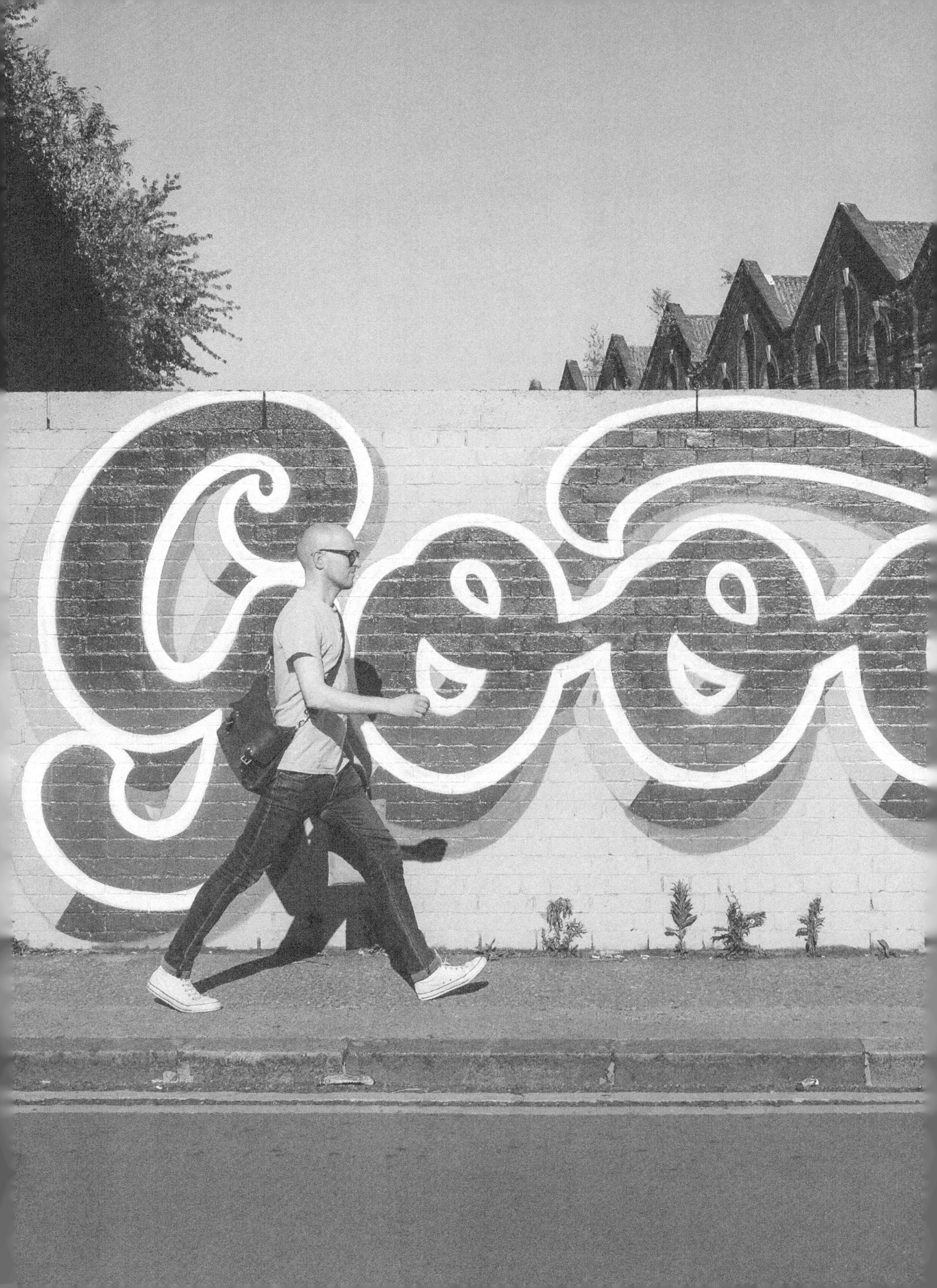

Do you know your worth? I mean not just in dollars and cents but what your time and energy is worth? I used to think the dollars equated to my value. In my experience I have learned that the value of being in a good place with my energy and mindset is worth a lot more dollars than I could ever imagine. So as you negotiate for that salary, make sure you are factoring in all the other aspects of your worth in that new job to make sure you are getting the full value of what is important to you.

You know when you are almost done... key word is 'almost'. Almost done is not the same as done. While it is close... it isn't the same. Often I find there are many reasons why I am 'almost'... insert any word here... ready, finished, confident, happy, accomplished. When I reflect on what gets in my way it is often my own fear... fear of failure, fear of starting, fear of things not working out... which are all stories are making up in my head. When I do finally act, beautiful things happen. So give up on the 'almost' and get going.

Find the Right Now Role 131

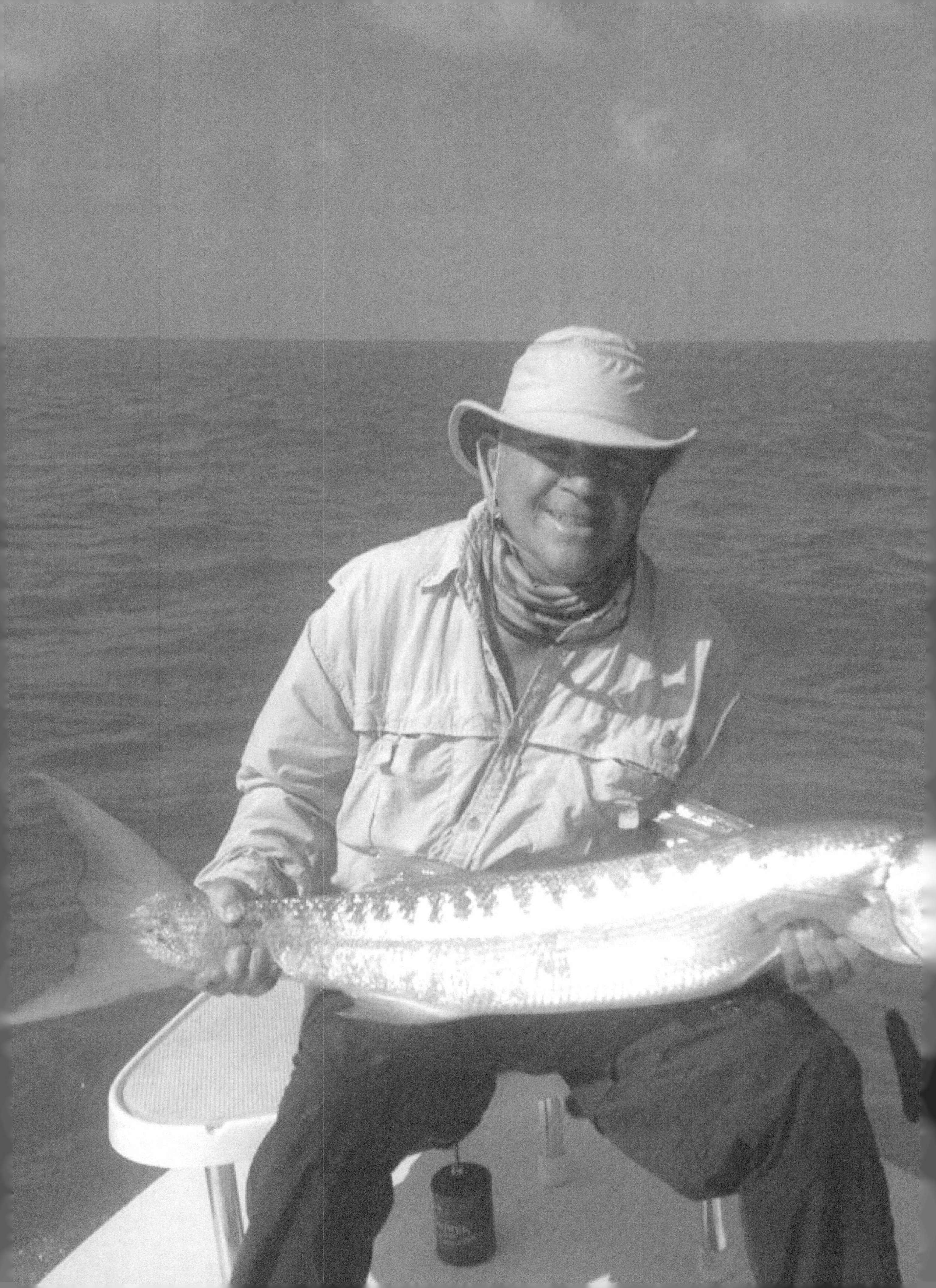

This guy gives the best advice... today he told me... I don't understand how some people go backwards going forwards. Just sit with that for a minute!?! It is true... I have learned sometimes by pushing forward I only set myself back. But if I take the time to pause and have patience to sort out the details successful progress is made. Out of the mouth of Dad today came great advice and wanted to pass it along.

Are you curious? I have learned the quality of my life equates to my ability to ask questions of myself and others. When I have the courage to lead with an open mind and ask questions, the options in front of me are more abundant and exciting. Where today can you be a good little monkey and be curious?

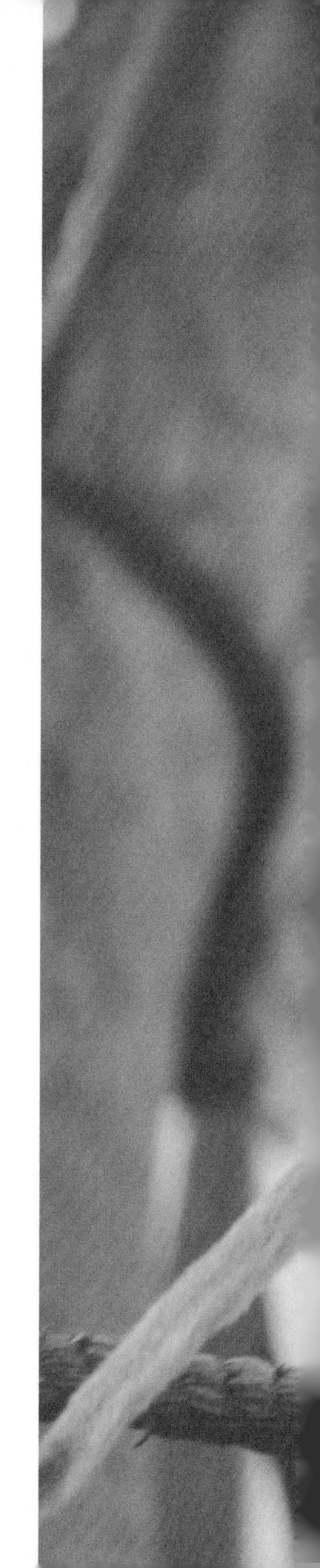

Find the Right Now Role   135

Day 1 would be an eye opener. When was your last, first day? New technology, new process, new people, new culture and just about new everything. But guess what isn't new... you and your leadership... so take a breath because you got this!

Find the Right Now Role 137

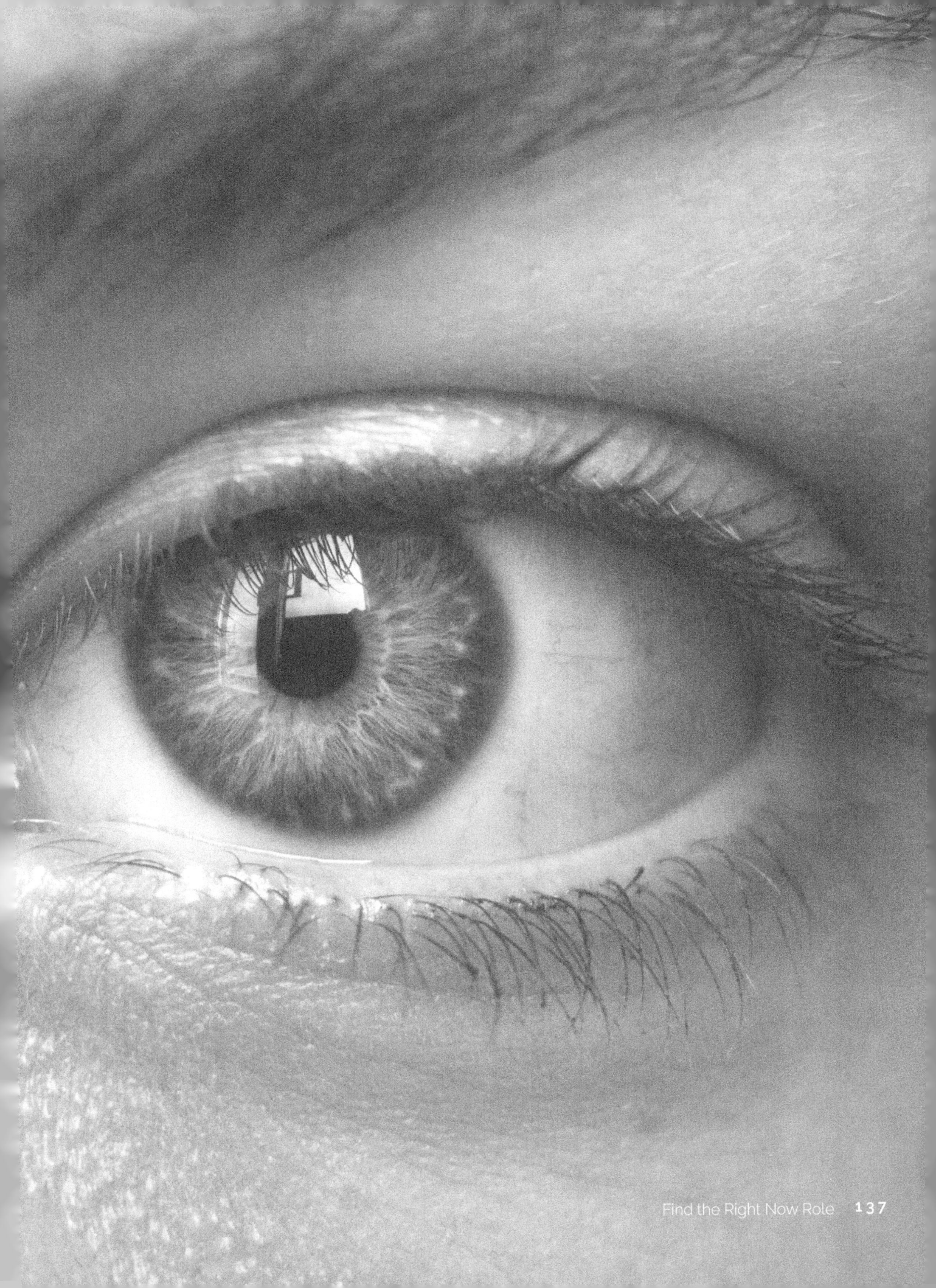

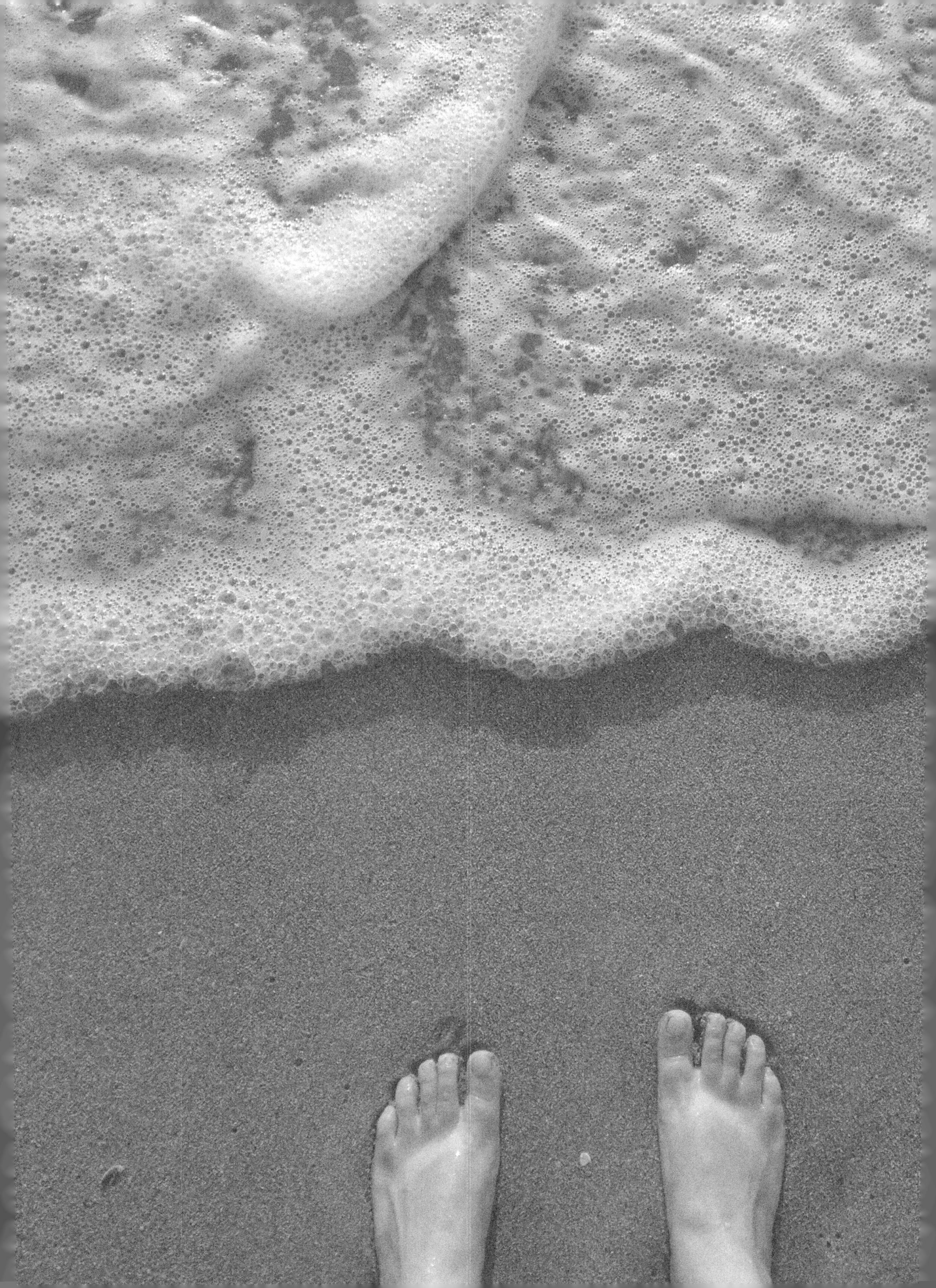

You can jump right back into it! I am energized and empowered to jump in with two feet. I love getting in the middle of things where help is needed and it is a great way to learn.

What is for me won't miss me.
How great of a thought is that?
How often do we think that we are missing
the opportunity or missing out chance.
When I believe that the things that are meant
for me will show up (no matter what) it is a powerful
thought... and the most amazing things show up
and take shape.

Find the Right Now Role

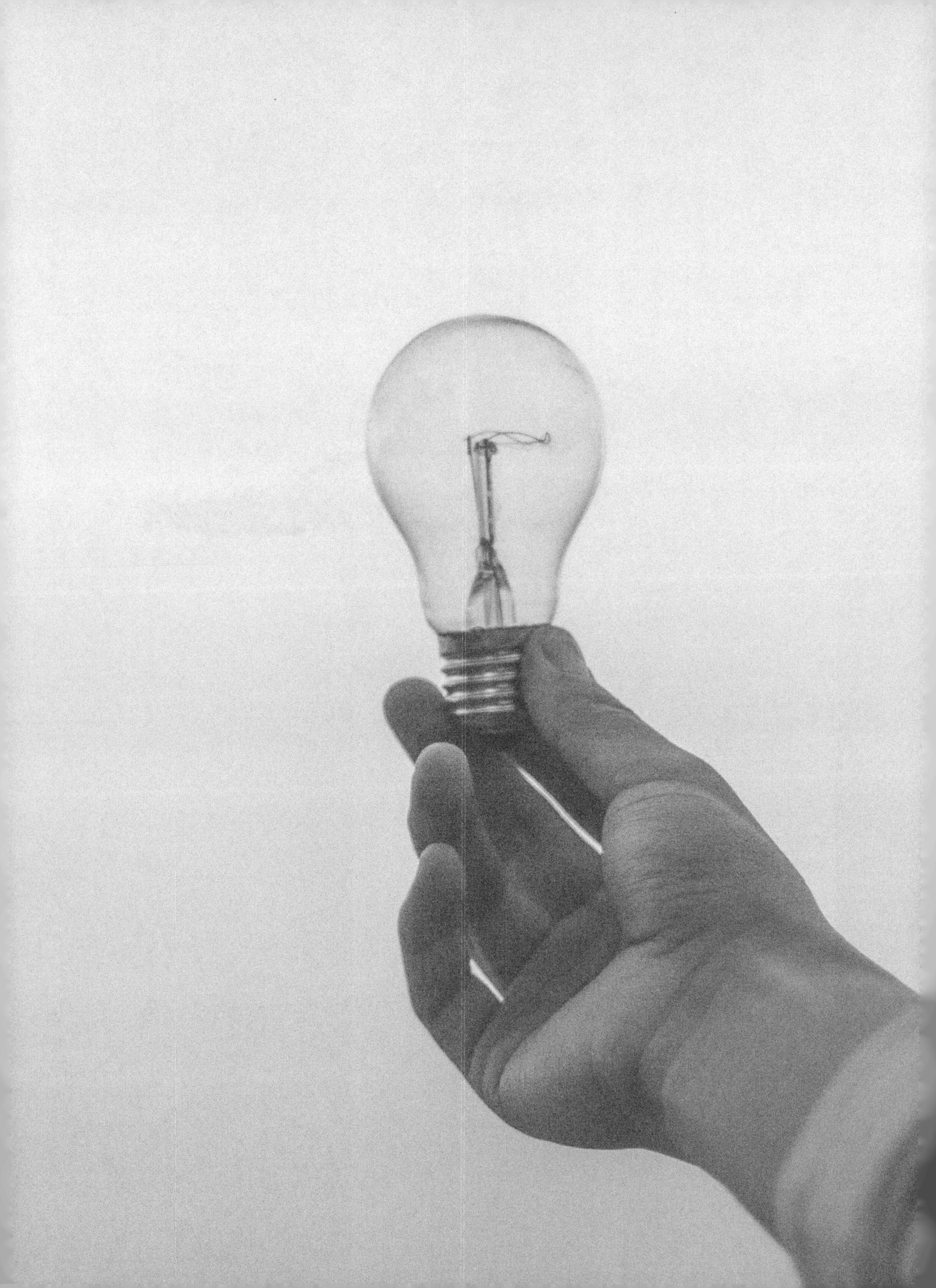

90 days into the new role... where did the time go? I now start to drink the koolaid regularly from this point forward. I am less 'new'... .more grounded and comfortable with voicing my opinion and perspective. I am learning my space and filling it to bring observations and ideas forward. I am also reflecting on what we have accomplished so far and excited for the plans ahead.

Some days feel like this mountain looks... far away, cold, high and you may resonate with 'who goes up there and why?'

But do you know what else this mountain is... closer than you think, only cold if you wear bad clothes, accessible by chair lift and ME - I go there! This view reminded me that reframing my perspective can change the daunting to spectacular. As I look at the next mountain or challenge ahead, I am reminded that one step at a time and with the right 'lifts' of support around me... I will get there.

Find the Right Now Role

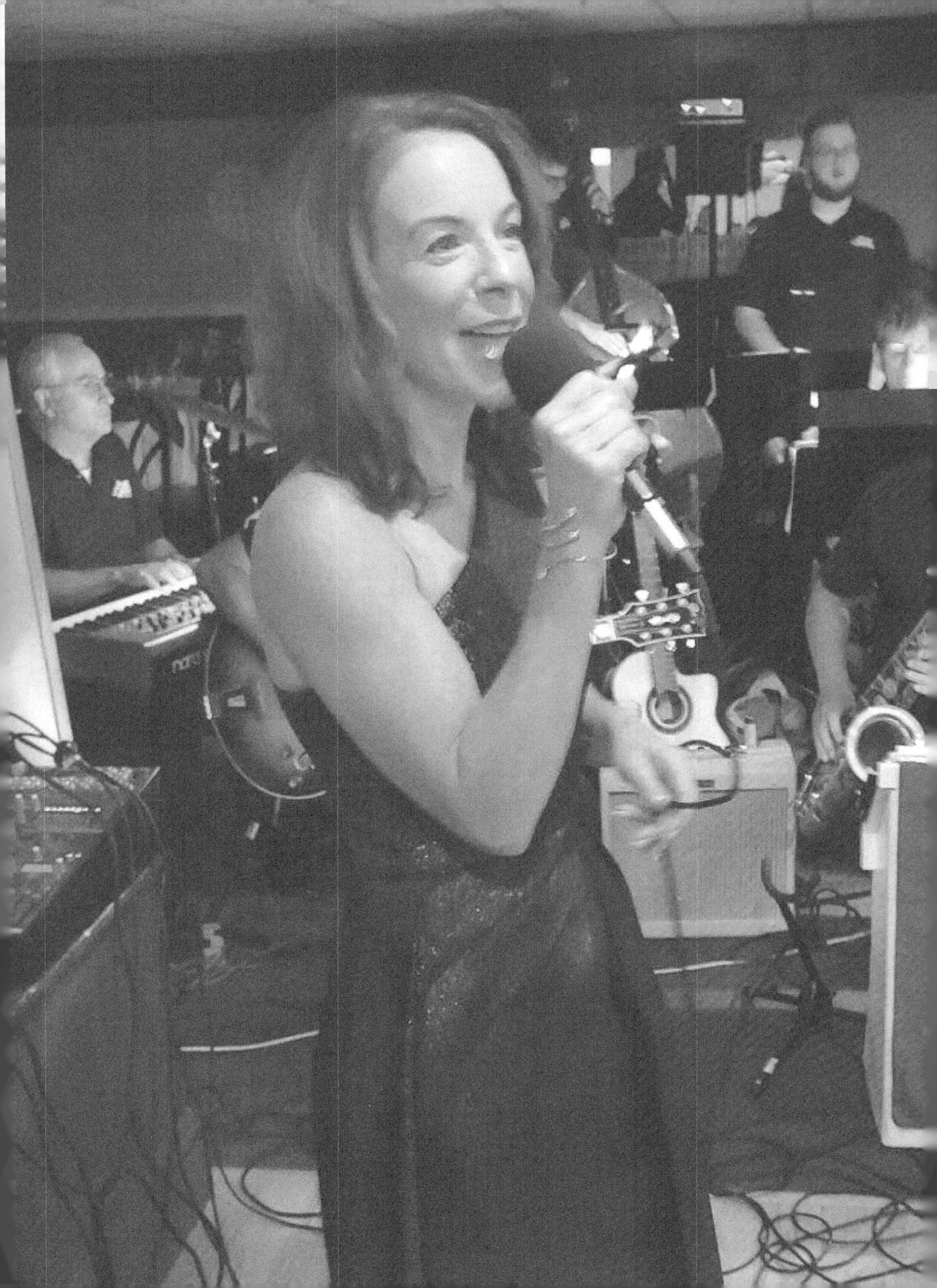

Everyone can benefit from voice lessons... like any other skill to get from good to great I know I need to work at it. But what I have also started working on is that other 'voice'... you know the one... the annoying, noisy one inside your head....we all have one.

I have begun training this voice with practice and exercises to feel when it sounds right. At first it so much work... trying to remember every little thing to make it better 'reframe, breathe, imagine'... all the same as singing.

I know one day I will stop having to think first, stop treating it like an exercise, and that day when it just happens without me thinking about it....oh I am so excited for that day.

Til then I will practices my ooo's and ah's... and remind myself that like my singing voice... my range is improving even if I don't see it yet.

I have learned there are times in leadership where I need to rip off the bandaid. The sore spot was healed enough, it was time to give it some air to fully heal and there was no need to protect it and cover it up anymore.

I have learned my old beliefs can be that sore spot. While I have wanted to protect them so as not to 'open up old wounds', I know that by exposing my true and authentic self I can miraculously heal to become a new and improved version of me.

And the scars dissolve faster too...

Find the Right Now Role 149

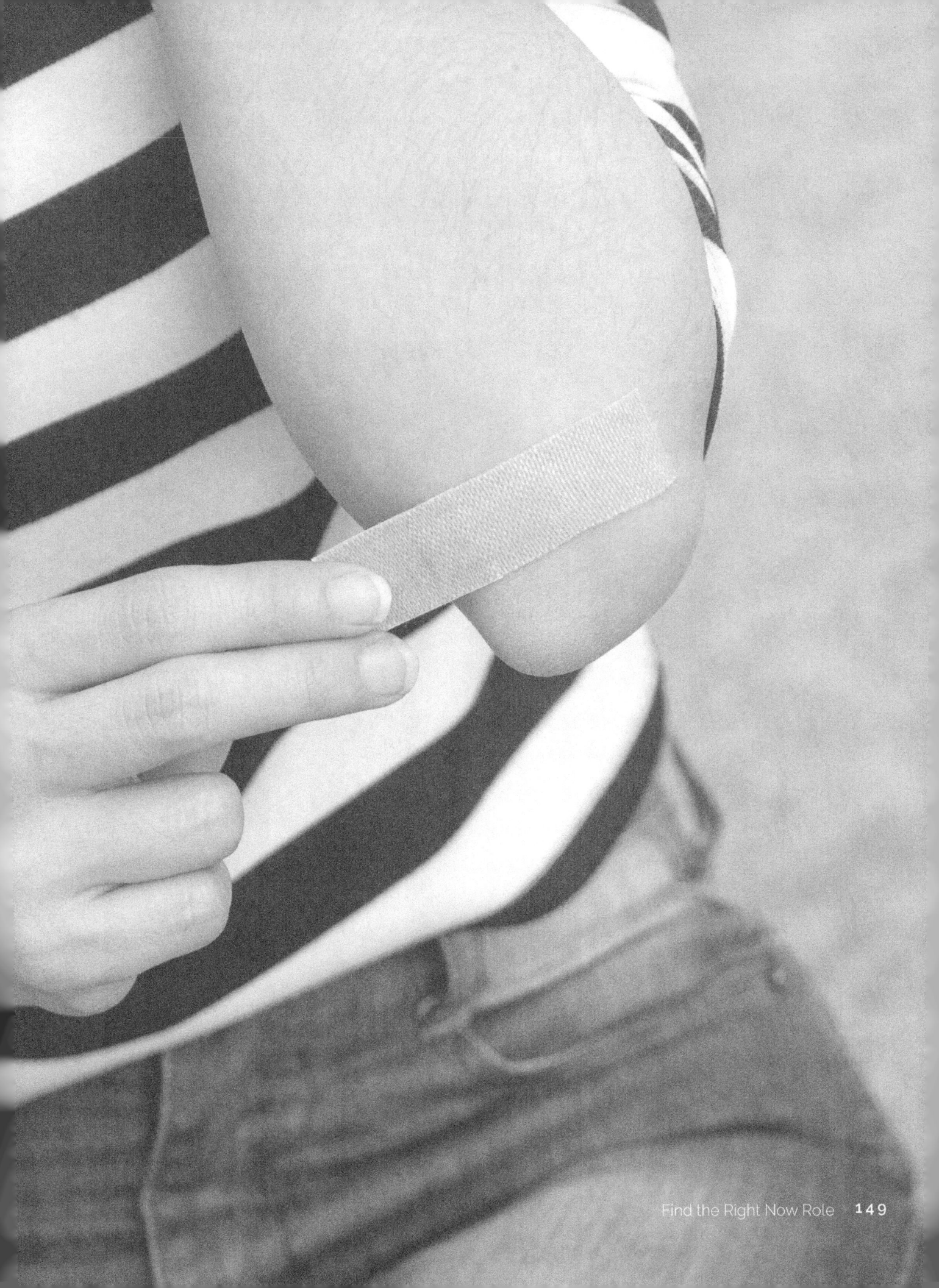

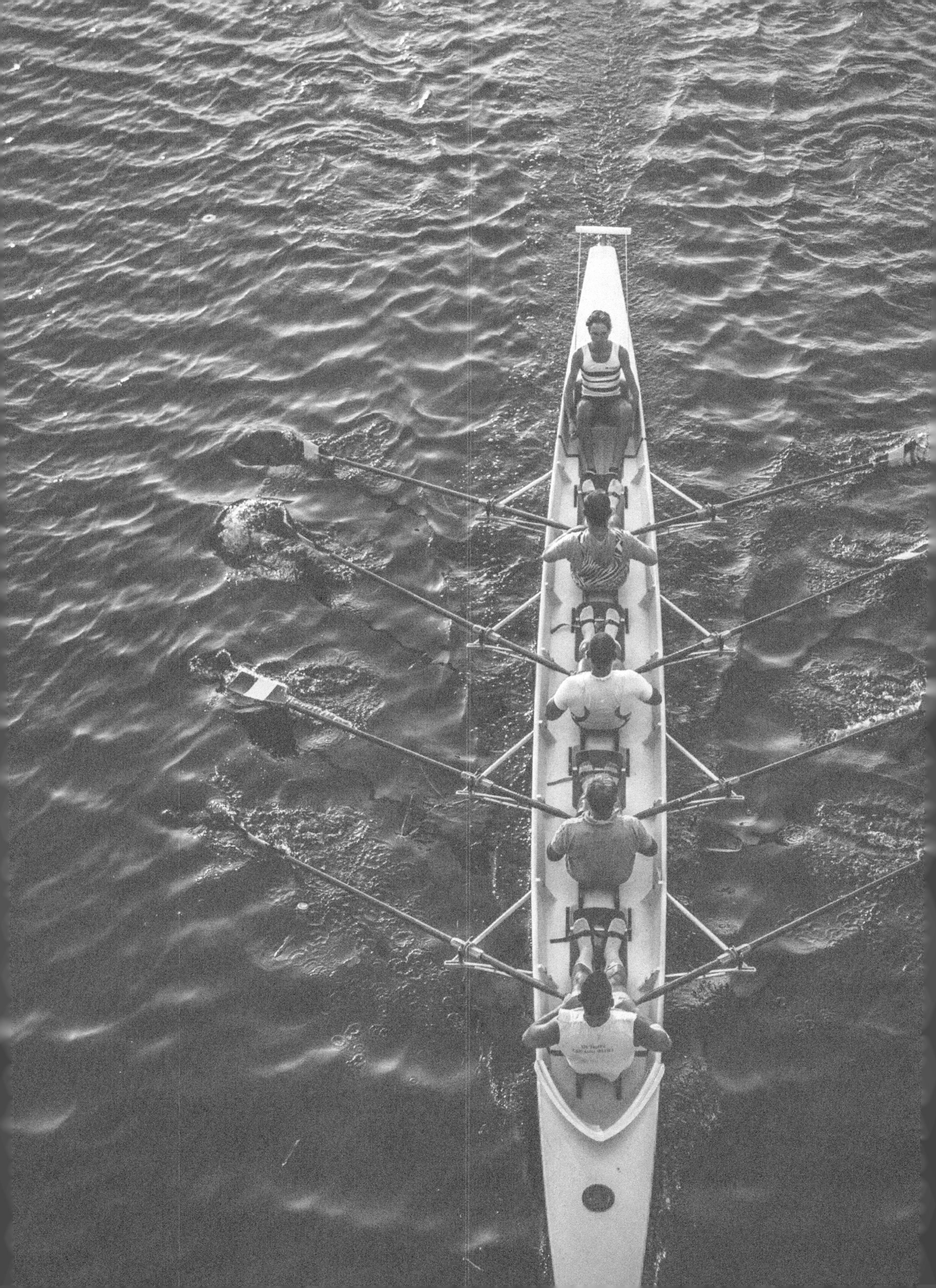

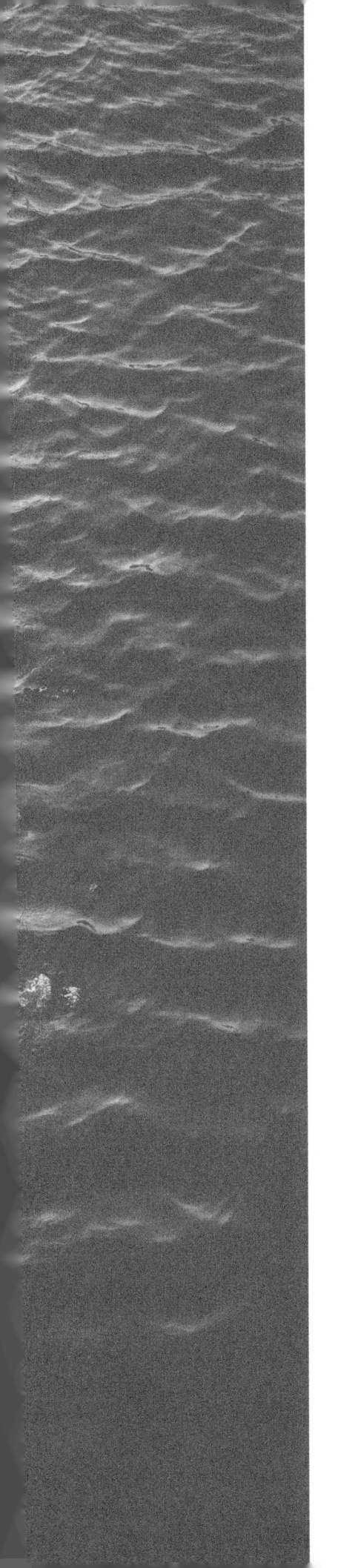

Take a page out of your own book... for me that is literal. Good reminder that not just what I do as a leader matters but how I do it. Some days the 'how' needs to outweigh the what. Reminding myself that is a-okay. I value my ability as a leader to lead people... some of my greatest bosses role modeled that for me and I hope to do that for others.

Stop thinking this will be like the last job. Read that again (or ten times). Often I catch myself... nothing is the same, nothing will feel the same and isn't that such a fabulous opportunity to grow in so many new ways!

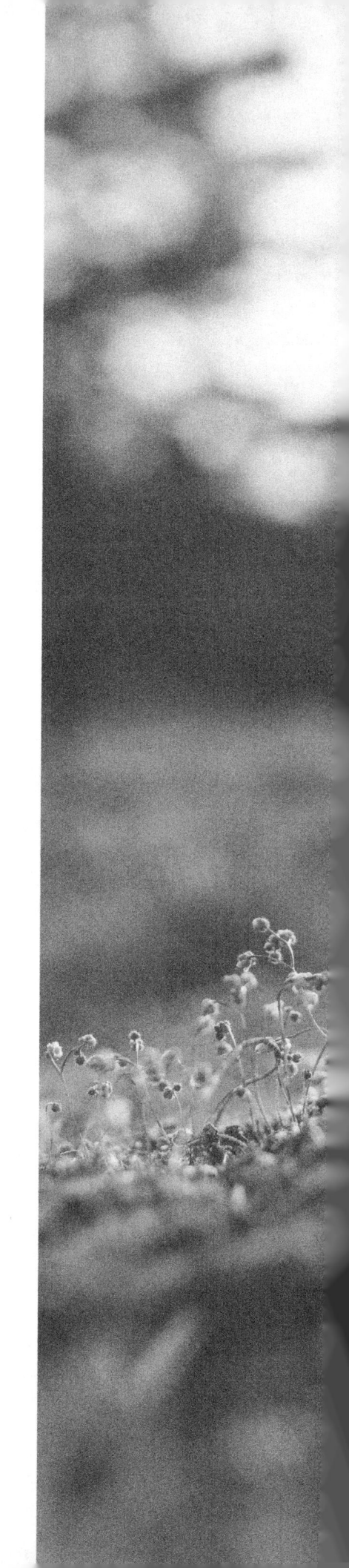

Find the Right Now Role

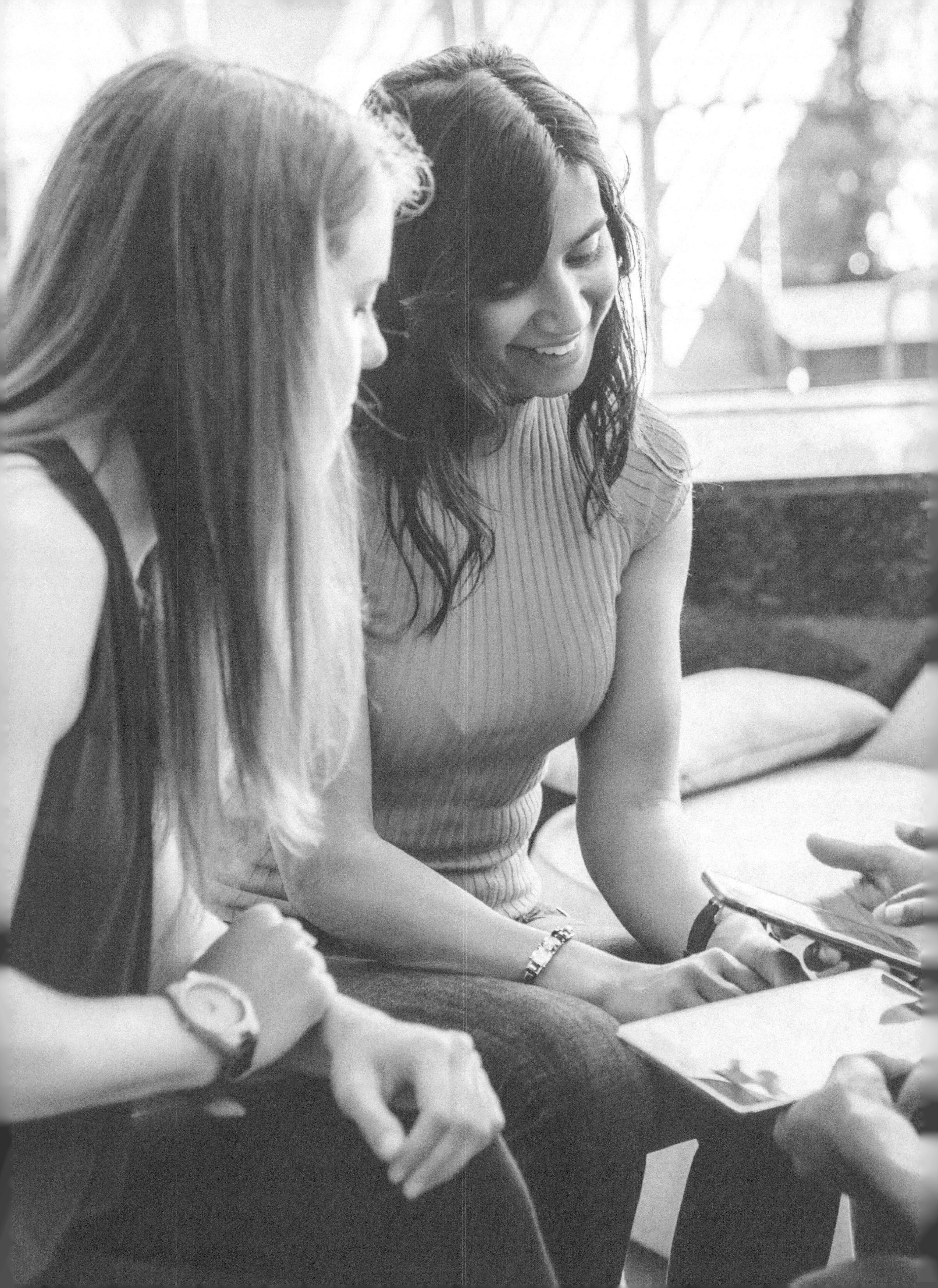

Keep on networking! Why would I need to do that? I have a job. How about that stronger network that was built over your career journey? How about others that can benefit from your experience? Just like leading, job searching is a skill… and you have mastered this one… so put it to good use and 'pay it forward'.

Don't disappear from your online network.
'Where did you go?' she asks.
'What do you mean? I'm right here.' I say.
'No, you disappeared.' she says.
My sister was referring to my presence on LinkedIn.
I guess she isn't wrong. I had been a little busy...
busy learning a new team, learning a new business
and planning for what is ahead. But she brought up
a good point. It took me time to get comfortable
with being present 'here' and finding my voice... so I
vowed not to give that up. So sister... you can't miss
me because I didn't go anywhere... and actually in
where I am headed I have found myself.

Find the Right Now Role

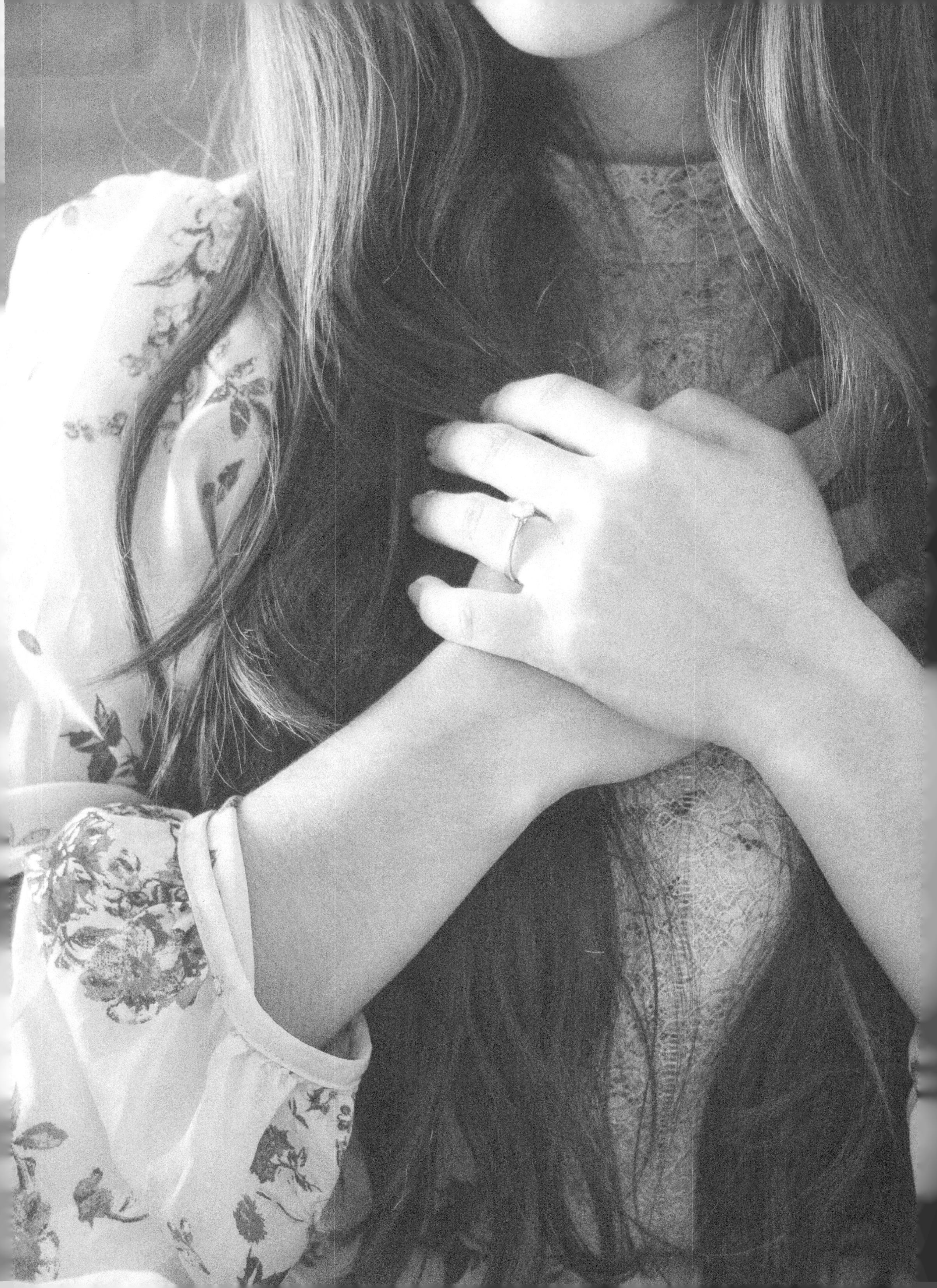

Are you really listening? I don't mean with your head or your ears but with your heart.

I have learned when I truly stop and listen with my heart - things sound different. While there are situations where my brain goes into overdrive to find an answer, I know when I step back and just listen to my heart there is less noise, things become simpler and the answer or response is bright as day (and this works both in business and personally).

What can you hear differently today?

Your most valuable asset is life experience...
what if we stepped back and thought about the
whole package? Not just the roles you have
held, or the companies you have worked for,
the accomplishments you have achieved or the
relationships you have built... but all of it.
I am grateful to embrace and celebrate my life
experience. It isn't just one thing but the package
all together that creates who I am as a leader.
And I would do it all the same way to get to where
I am today.

Find the Right Now Role

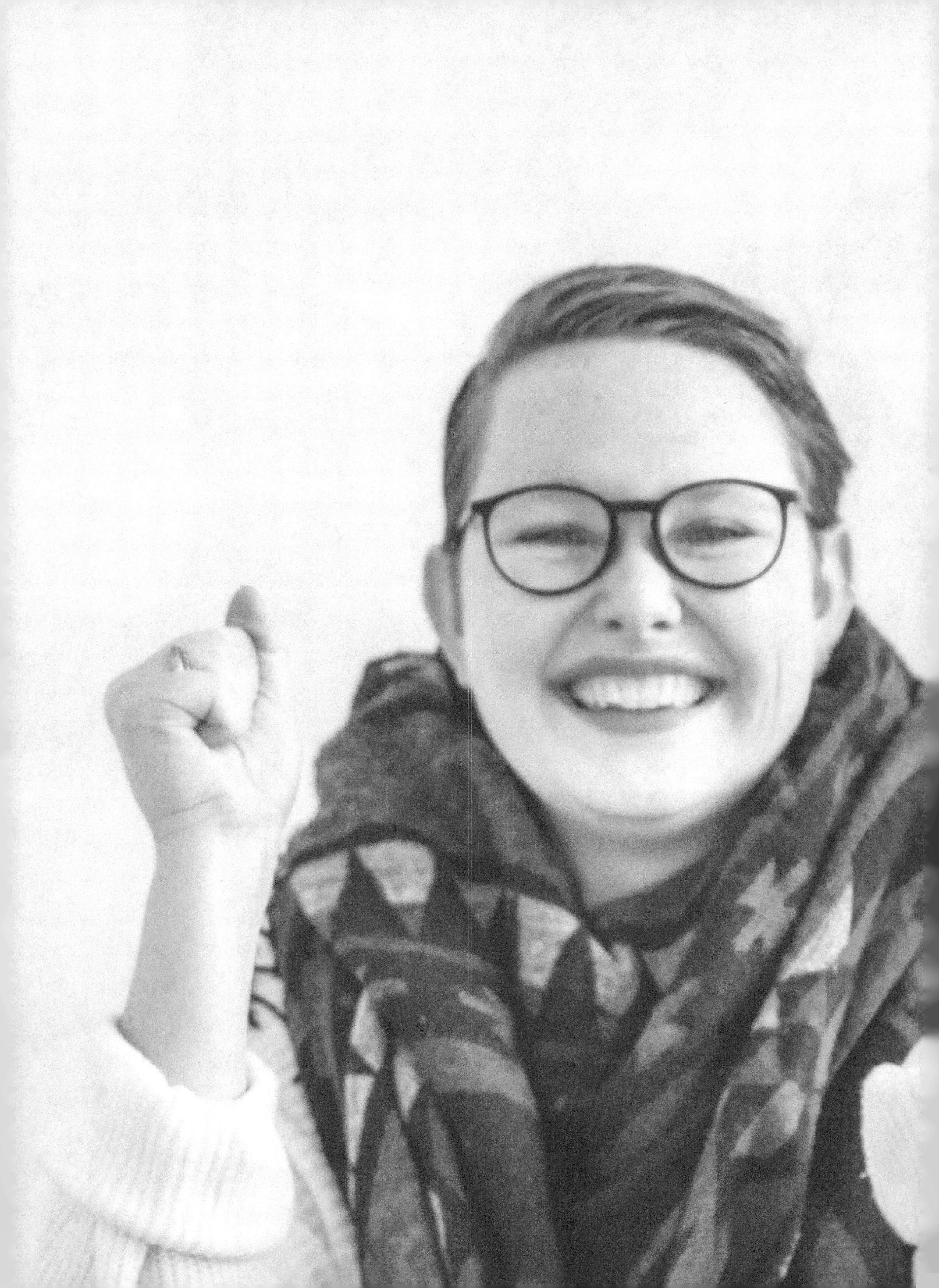

You will lose some things/people as you gain others. As I have shedded one part of my life and moved into another, I have let go of some things and people that no longer serve me. While it may be sad, it is refreshing to know I am moving into a new phase, a new beginning. I recently realized, I can't 'unsee' certain things and that has moved me forward whether I was ready or not. But what I am ready for is the excitement and anticipation of what is ahead, what is possible and what will come next!

Corporate lessons learned from band rehearsal...
I realized so many of these lessons translate to work life.

1. Practice may not make you perfect but it does create more confidence for when the wobbles happen... you can handle them better

2. A band like an organization has a culture - you need to figure out what works and align on how you can work best together

3. When you are in your zone and it just feels good - you know that is what you want more of! (My team and I talked about this just this week)

4. Sometimes things won't work and you need to decide how to pivot and adjust to get the results you want. Worst case - scrap the song (or project) and move on to another one.

5. Lastly... when you are doing what you love it doesn't feel like work!

Find the Right Now Role

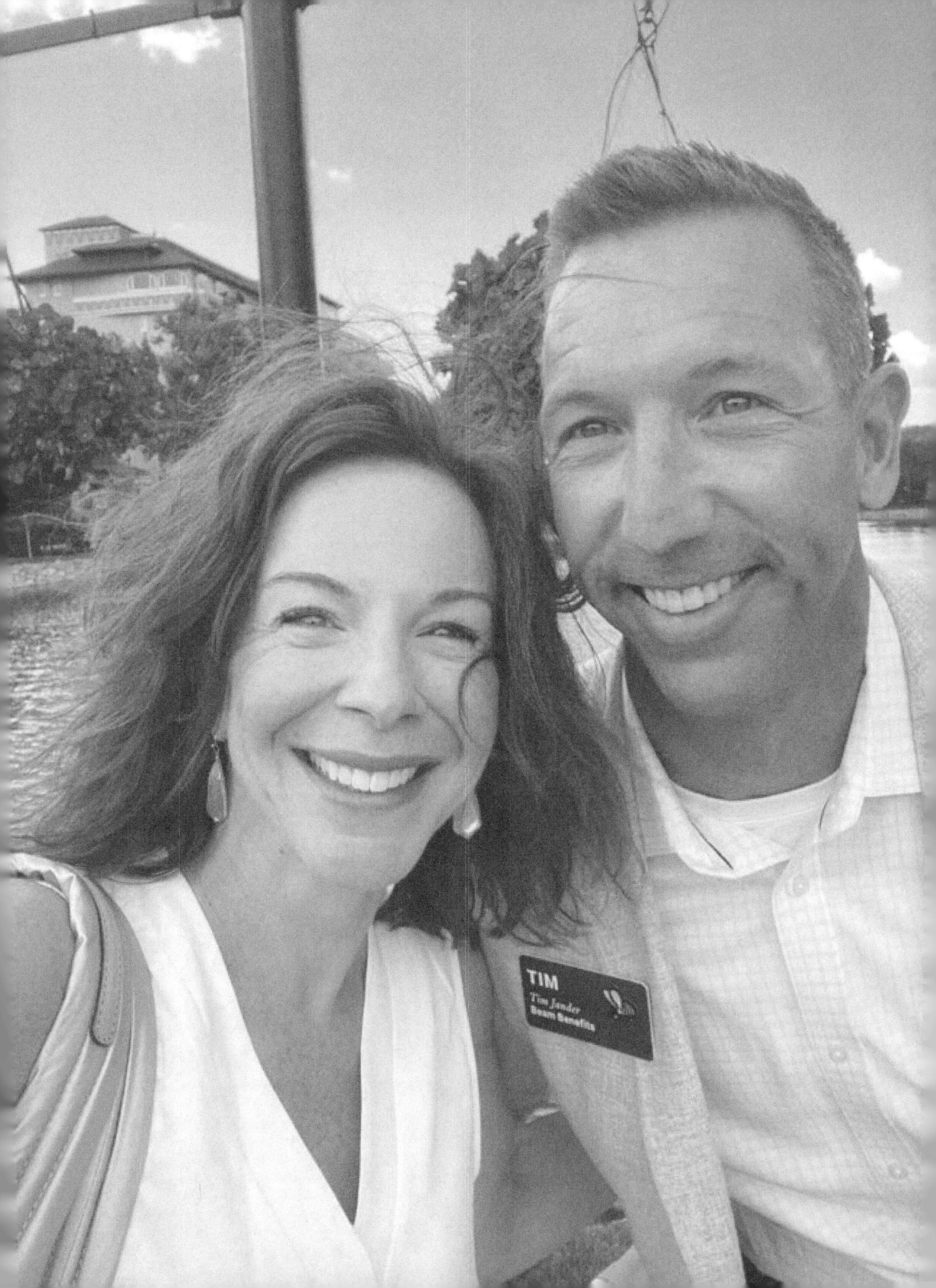
TIM

As my career has progressed, learned the value of memories and relationships that have become much sweeter overtime. Thankful for my network that is always there for me!

I have learned the beauty of having a posse to rely on. Reminds me that my work posse is just as valuable... in the times to celebrate, the times to buckle up and get to work and the times when I need to be supported and heard. Thankful for my posse that makes every day a fabulous ride.

Find the Right Now Role 169

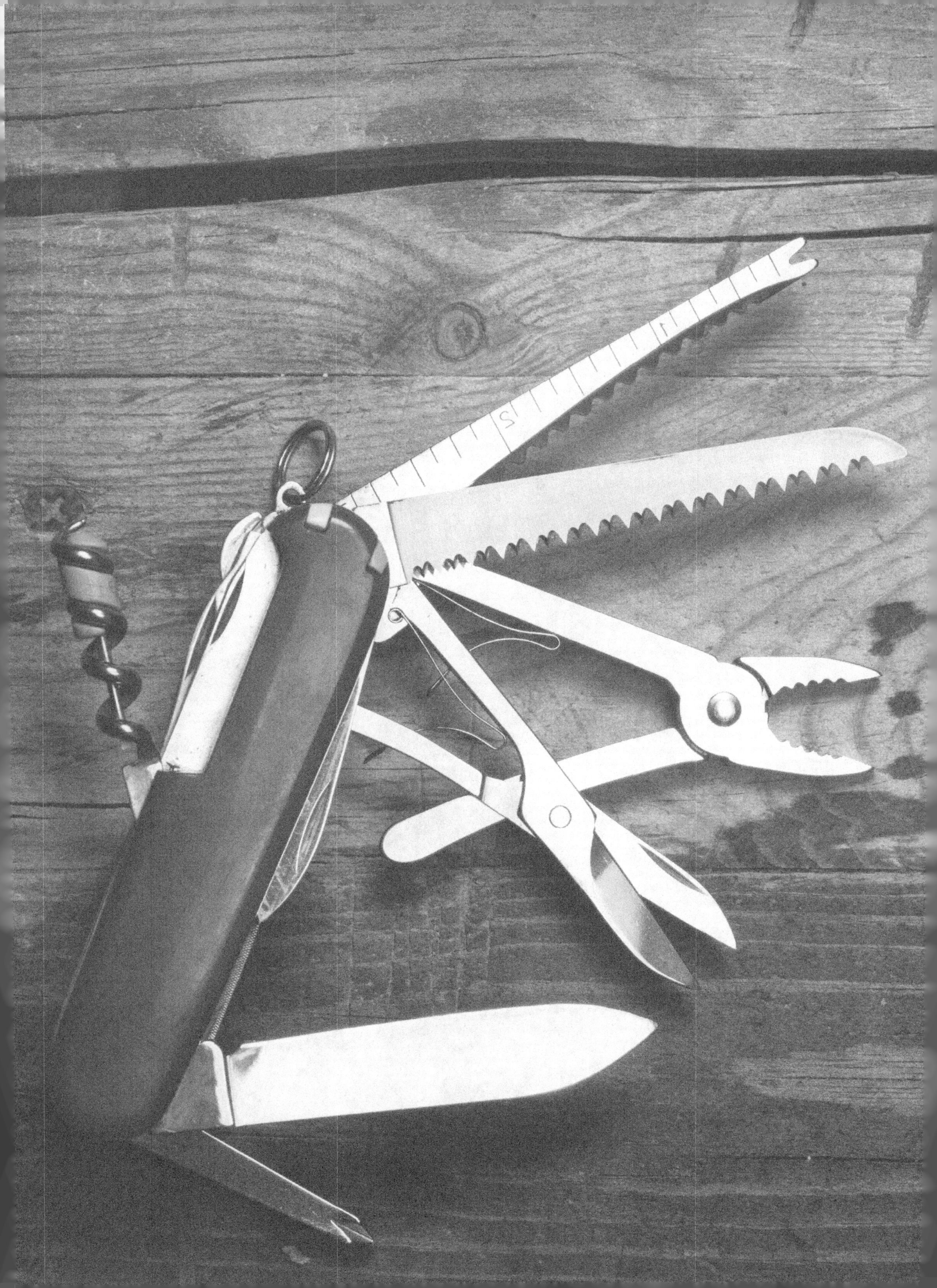

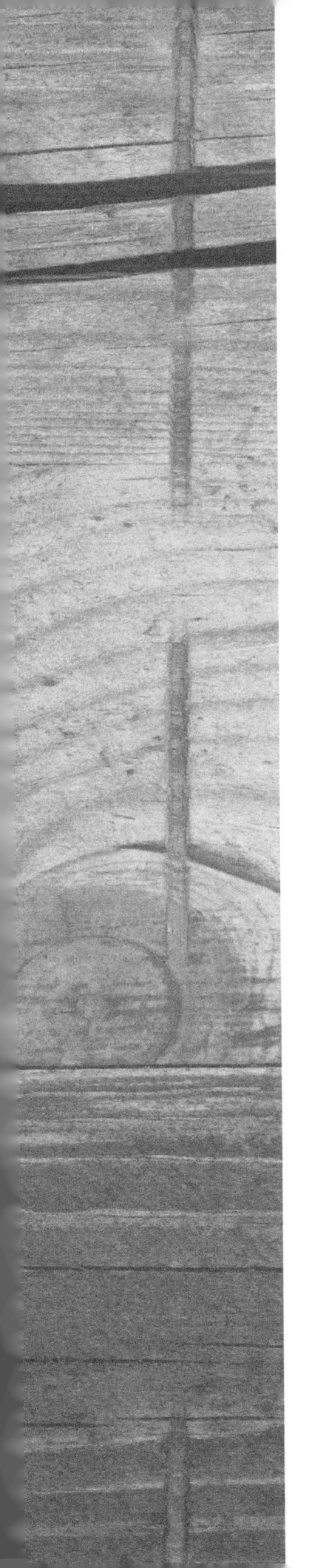

Over the course of my career, I have learned the importance of being flexible in how I use my multi-faceted skills. While some days are the cork screw, others may be the bottle opener. Each is important but for different purposes….the key is knowing when to use which tool for which purpose. Not to mention some days it is fun to break out a tool you haven't used in awhile.

When was the last time you were the Swiss Army knife?

What happens when you thought what was the North Star isn't? For me, I take a beat to wallow in my disappointment, frustration, fear and sadness. And then I find my gratitude... my appreciation that what wasn't for me has moved out of my way to make way for something new... which will be this or better!

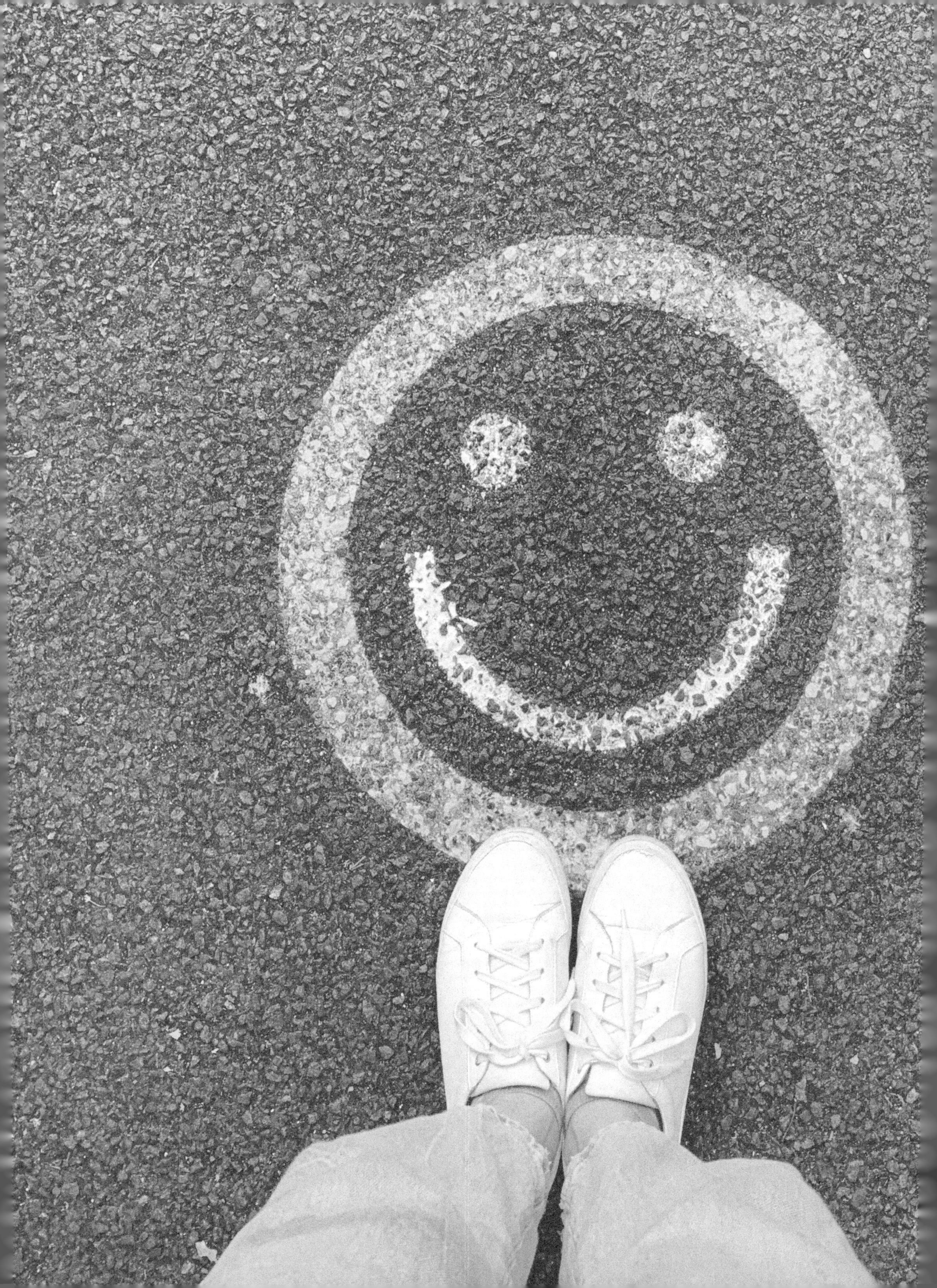

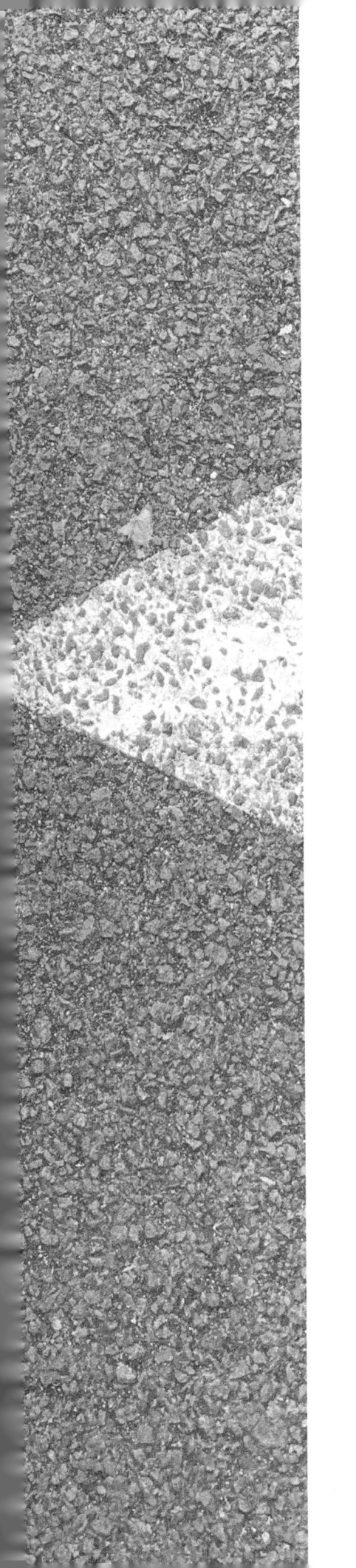

Can you stand on your own two feet?
I spend a lot of time focused on my
physical ability to have a strong core so I can
stay on my own two feet.
In my past, my career has often propped up my self
worth... gave me a sense that I was valuable. I have
learned that when my core strength and belief in
myself is strong enough I don't need to rely on my
career as a prop. I can successfully stand on my
own in all ways.

Do you lead in the rest of your life like you do business? With joy, and not judgment with curiosity and not criticism? Are you part of the solution versus part of the problem? I have learned that the same approaches to succeed in leading at work can apply beautifully in the rest of my life... when I remember to use them. How can you apply a leadership skill to the rest of your life today?

Find the Right Now Role · 177

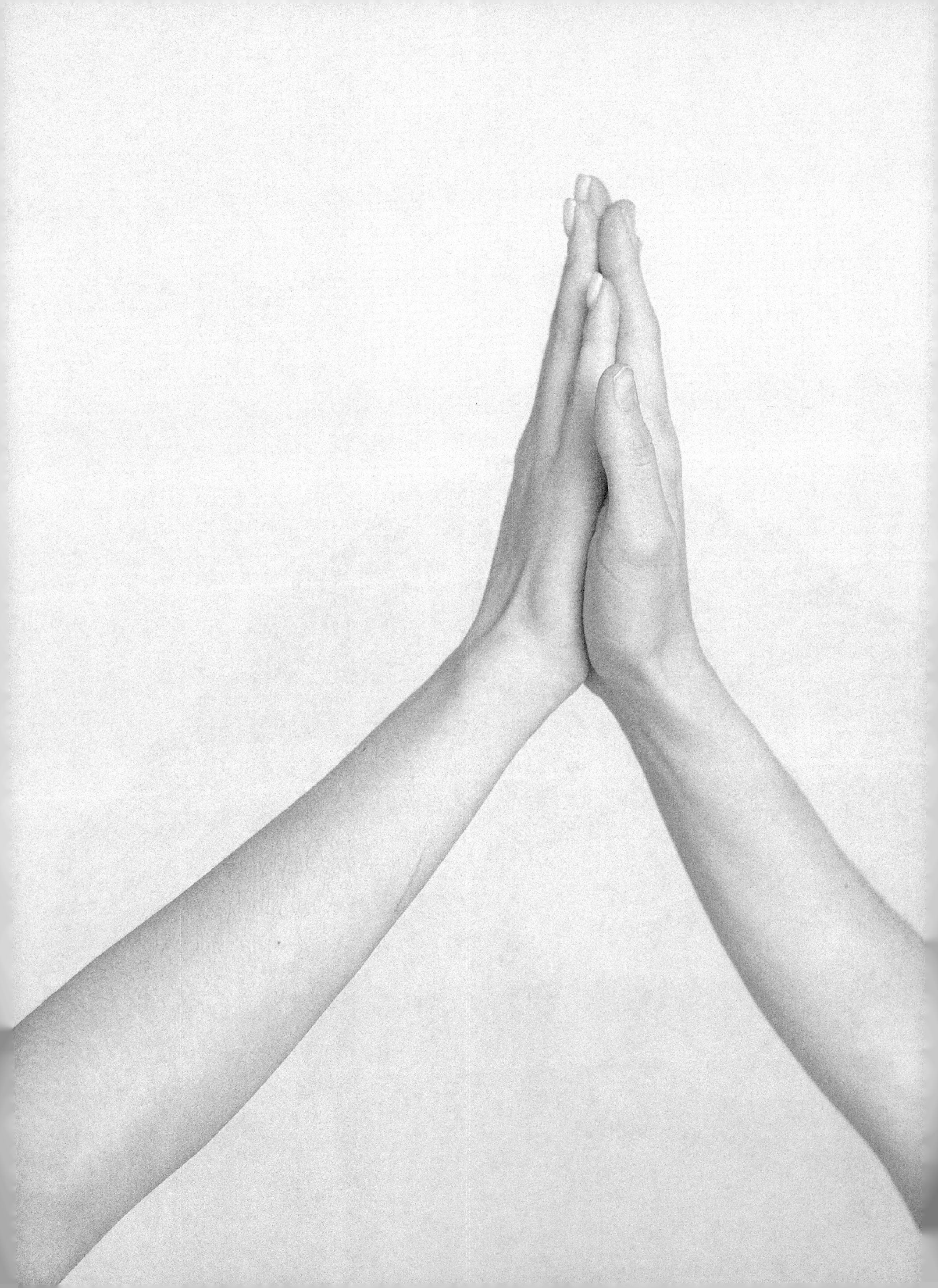

Are you irreplaceable? I used to think I should be... be the only person who can do my job and have job security! But with that usually comes a lack of process and effective working environment across the team. Also people don't always learn how to make decisions without you. Instead I have learned to grow and coach my team to think how I think and do what I do so if I wasn't here they would be a-okay without me. Much more rewarding place to be and keeps all your own personal options open for the future!

In business, we talk often about managing
to outcomes and results. While I am a big believer
in this, I have learned as I think about my career
it is the journey that matters more than the
destination... am I growing, am I learning,
am I expanding and transforming. If the answer
is yes, I know there is value in the role I am in.

When I think about my family, I am proud
of how we have grown and transformed together.
Excited about the journey we are on and wish
you all the best for yours!

Find the Right Now Role 181

Made in the USA
Middletown, DE
20 January 2024